EMIGRATING to...

NEW ZEALAND

Visit our How To website at **www.howto.co.uk**

At **www.howto.co.uk** you can engage in conversation with our authors – all of whom have 'been there and done that' in their specialist fields. You can get access to special offers and additional content but, most importantly, you will be able to engage with, and become a part of, a wide and growing community of people just like yourself.

At **www.howto.co.uk** you'll be able to talk to, and share tips with, people who have similar interests and are facing similar challenges in their lives. People who, just like you, have the desire to change their lives for the better – be it through moving to a new country, starting a new business, growing their own vegetables, or writing a novel.

At **www.howto.co.uk** you'll find the support and encouragement you need to help make your aspirations a reality.

You can go direct to **www.emigrating-to-new-zealand.co.uk** which is part of the main How To site.

How To Books strives to present authentic,
inspiring, practical information in their books.
Now, when you buy a title from **How To Books**,
you get even more than just words on a page.

EMIGRATING to...

NEW ZEALAND

Comprehensive, practical information about the emigration process and life in the other down under

STEVE HORRELL

howto books

Published by How To Books Ltd
Spring Hill House, Spring Hill Road,
Begbroke, Oxford OX5 1RX, United Kingdom
Tel: (01865) 375794 Fax: (01865) 379162
info@howtobooks.co.uk
www.howtobooks.co.uk

Photo credits: **x**, © Rick Carlson – Fotolia.com; **10**, © Gina Smith – Fotolia.com;
22, © Dmitry Kudryavtsev – Fotolia.com; **38**, © OlgaLIS – Fotolia.com; **64**, © Giles Lewis;
72, © Lasse Kristensen – Fotolia.com; **79**, © Chris Hellyar – Fotolia.com; **80**, © Andrew
Martin – Fotolia.com; **86**, © CJPhoto – Fotolia.com; **98**, © Michael Flippo – Fotolia.com;
108, © Jacom Stephens – iStock.com **123**, © Kelpfish – Fotolia.com; **124**, © Paulus Rusyanto –
Fotolia.com; **134**, © Stuart Corlett – Fotolia.com; **144**, © Christopher Hawey – Fotolia.com;
162, © knoppers – Fotolia.com; **175**, © Lai Leng Yiap – Fotolia.com; **21, 85, 133, 143,
166, 174, 180** © specialist publishing services ltd

First published 2006
Reprinted 2007
Reprinted with updates 2008
Second edition 2010

British Library Cataloguing in Publication Data
A catalogue record for this book is available from
the British Library.

ISBN: 978 1 84528 398 8

Produced for How To Books by Deer Park Productions, Tavistock
Typeset by specialist publishing services ltd, Montgomery
Cover design by Baseline Arts Ltd, Oxford
Printed and bound by Cromwell Press Group, Trowbridge, Wiltshire

Note: The material contained in this book is set out in good
faith for general guidance and no liability can be accepted
for loss or expense incurred as a result of relying in particular
circumstances on statements made in the book. The laws and
regulations are complex and liable to change, and readers should
check the current position with the relevant authorities before
making personal arrangements.

Contents

Preface   ix

1   **Introducing New Zealand**   1
History   1
Geography   2
Trade and economy   4
Climate   5
Lifestyle and people   6
Facts and figures   9

2   **Why Emigrate?**   11
What factors?   11
Quality of life   12
Taxation   13
Job satisfaction   17
Politics   18
Making the decision   19
Culture shock   19

3   **Visa Application**   23
What job?   23
Skilled/business stream   26
Birth certificates   32
Police certificates   33
Medical certificates   34
Passports   35
Summary   36

4   **Emigration Preparations**   39
Spidergram   39
Selling your house   41
Removal company   43
Household and electrical equipment   46
Vehicles   52
TV licence   54
Insurances   54
Credit cards   58
Loyalty cards   58

Utility bills 59
Standing orders/direct debits 59
Pensions 60
Family credits and benefits 60
Inland Revenue 61
Bank accounts 62

5   Pets **65**
Export regulations 66
Budget 67
Transit kennels 68
Flight information 69
Arrival in New Zealand 70
Microchipping 71
Quarantine 71

6   Getting There **73**
Flight planning 73
UK travel 74
Personal clothing 74
Documents 75
Money 76
The LA experience 76
Hong Kong 78

7   Arrival in New Zealand **81**
Customs/MAF 81
Hotels and motels 83
Public transport 84

8   House Hunting and Buying **87**
Deciding where to live 87
Publications 88
Internet 88
Building inspections and reports 90
Legal process 92
Open home 95
Rental property 97

9   Education **99**
NCEA system 100
State schools 102
Private schools 105
Tertiary education 105

10	**Employment**	**109**
	What skills?	109
	Job vacancies	112
	Occupational registration	113
	Job hunting	114
	Job hunting tips	116
	Conclusion	118
11	**Health Issues**	**119**
	Doctors	119
	Dentists	121
	Chemists	122
12	**Cars and Driving**	**125**
	Driving licence	125
	Buying a car	128
	Insurance	129
	Driving in New Zealand	130
	Kiwi drivers	131
13	**General Information**	**135**
	Climate and weather	135
	Earthquakes	136
	Television and radio	138
	Entertainment	139
	Bars and pubs	139
	Eating out	140
14	**Major Cities and Regions**	**145**
	Northland	145
	Auckland	146
	Waikato	148
	Bay of Plenty	149
	Gisborne	150
	Taranaki	150
	Hawkes Bay	151
	Manawatu / Wanganui	151
	Wellington	152
	Marlborough	156
	Tasman	157
	West Coast	158
	Canterbury	158
	Otago	160
	Southland	161

15 **Final Thoughts**   **163**

16 **Kiwispeak**   **167**

17 **Event Planner**   **175**

    Index   **181**

Preface

There are many guidebooks available illustrating New Zealand and providing a mine of practical information, all of which can be considered as useful reading and an excellent source of reference. However, the idea for this book originated after a fruitless search for some sort of guide that would help to cope with the roller coaster ride that is the emigration process itself. It covers a wide range of topics and issues that will be encountered, from the discussion phase through to the initial settling period in New Zealand. This book is not a definitive process to gain a visa, more the way to approach the whole issue of emigration.

Facts and figures quoted in this book are accurate at the time of going to print but laws and procedures are forever changing. It is therefore absolutely essential to double-check vital information through an official source, particularly when dealing with visa and medical requirements. Information researched and written on a Friday could well have changed on the following Monday, particularly where government departments such as immigration, education and taxation both in the UK and New Zealand are involved.

Achieving the ultimate goal, to leave the shores of the UK and settle in New Zealand, was not a simple process for us. One of our favourite sayings, that must have been uttered twice a day for at least six months before we left, was *nobody said it was going to be easy*!

There are literally hundreds of hurdles that will need to be negotiated, sometimes on a daily basis, before leaving the UK and after arrival in New Zealand. It is highly likely that any potential immigrant will still need to carry on working in the months and weeks leading up to emigration, so patience, preparation and sound planning are the keys to success.

I hope this book will provide some inspiration in your quest to emigrate to New Zealand. At the very least it should help you acquire more of an understanding about what lies ahead and provide an insight into some of the issues that, had we been privy to beforehand, would have benefited us in our endeavours. Good luck.

Steve Horrell

1
Introducing New Zealand

HISTORY

The Polynesian Maori reached New Zealand in about AD 950, but it was not until 1840 that the chieftains entered into a contract with Britain and ceded sovereignty to Queen Victoria. This contract is known as the Treaty of Waitangi, which is celebrated by way of a public holiday in New Zealand every year. The treaty outlines three main points:

- The Government makes law.

- Maori resources and way of life are protected.

- The basic rights of *all* people within New Zealand are protected.

In 1975 the Treaty of Waitangi Act was passed by Parliament and the Waitangi Tribunal was formed to consider Maori land claims. The 1840 Treaty remains controversial to this day as the original Maori and English versions were different, and it is said that virtually all of the 50 Maori chiefs who put their names to the document did not truly understand what they were signing.

It was also in 1840 that the British declared New Zealand a colony, to quell the unruly conditions and the concerns of missionaries over friction with the Maori in the sealing and whaling industries.

New Zealand is still part of the British Commonwealth, although there is a growing band of people in the country who believe that the national flag should be changed in favour of something more representative of the nation as a whole. The Silver Fern features prominently on prototype flags, but the Union Jack does not. This should not be misconstrued as a sign of New Zealand aiming to gain recognition as a republic – at least not yet – although there is seemingly growing support for such a move in the future, which some say will happen in the next ten years.

GEOGRAPHY

Many people believe that New Zealand consists of a 'couple of insignificant islands just off the coast of Australia'. This is far from the truth, although most Aussies you meet will try to convince you otherwise! Located in the South Pacific Ocean, New Zealand is some 1,600 kilometres east of Australia across the Tasman Sea – about three hours' flying time from Wellington to Sydney.

New Zealand is made up not just of the North and South Islands. Other groups governed from Wellington include the Bounty, Campbell, Chatham and Kermadec Islands.

The combined size of these land areas is slightly larger than the UK. About 60 per cent of the North and South Islands ranges between 200 and over 1,000 metres above sea level and the country has more than 220 named mountains exceeding 2,300 metres in height. To give that some perspective, Ben Nevis in Scotland is a mere 1,300 metres.

The country is volcanic, particularly so in parts of the North Island where geysers and geo-thermal activity are an impressive tourist attraction. A volcanic range in the north central region has three 'active' peaks of which Mount Ruapehu is the highest at 2,800 metres. The South Island boasts snow-covered mountains, glacial-formed lakes and fiords, and wide expanses of arable land along the east coast.

Fig. 1. Location map of New Zealand.

TRADE AND ECONOMY

Over the past 20 years, New Zealand has built itself an industrialised, free market economy that can easily compete with many other nations across the world. The positive side of this is the boost in 'real' incomes, although many at the bottom of the salary ladder appear to have been left behind, whilst the technological capabilities of the industrial sector as a whole have grown.

In line with world trends, New Zealand is reliant on trade – particularly in the agricultural market – to promote growth. Like many other countries, it has been affected by economic slowdown coupled with the general fall in global commodity prices. The need to diversify its output in order to compete in world markets saw New Zealand grasp the opportunity to expand its expertise in agricultural research, animal and crop technology and it is now recognised as a world-class performer, using its land to the greatest possible advantage. Its wines are acknowledged as some of the world's best, and major exports are made to the USA, Asia and Europe.

Despite 85 per cent of its population living in cities or large towns, the main export earnings are raised from farm produce and over 60 per cent of the total land area is utilised by the farming industry. The climate of the North Island is ideal for growing sub-tropical varieties of fruit and grapes while the South Island features fertile land for dairy cattle grazing and cereal crops.

Who could write a book on New Zealand and not mention sheep? There are over 45 million sheep in the country – more than ten times the human population. Add to this nearly five million cattle, 1.5 million goats and 500,000 pigs and there is certainly no shortage of items to accommodate a great Kiwi pastime, the barbecue. Incidentally, some New Zealanders do not appreciate jokes about themselves and sheep, so good advice is to steer clear of the subject or run the risk of upsetting somebody!

CLIMATE

The geographical position of New Zealand in the South Pacific perhaps conjures up images of palm trees, grass skirts and beaches. In reality, the weather in New Zealand is far from tropical and can be described as variable to the extreme. The north of the North Island is actually sub-tropical while the southernmost tip of the South Island has nothing standing between it and the Antarctic.

In any one day, the weather can change from rain, hail or snow to warm sunshine. There is nothing worse than being caught out so, when travelling around the country, people tend to layer their clothing. Overall, New Zealand has a moderate climate and the winter months certainly do not seem as dull and grey as those experienced across the UK! The weather chart below graphically illustrates the average temperature range.

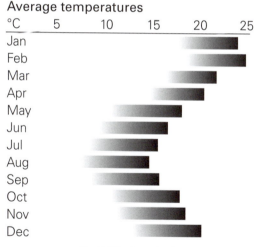

Fig. 2. Weather chart.

New Zealand is known for its extremely high UV rating because the clean air and environment make the sun stronger and harsh. There is also a documented occurrence of a hole in the earth's ozone layer that sits above the country, causing the suns rays to have a greater and quicker effect than in other parts of the world.

LIFESTYLE AND PEOPLE

New Zealand is very much an outdoor lifestyle country, which is understandable given the wide expanse of undeveloped countryside and coastline that can be explored in many ways. Mountain biking, tramping (hiking), boating and fishing seem to be the most popular pastimes and are all very much family oriented. The short drive of no more than 20 minutes from the Central Business District (CBD) of Wellington to the middle of native bush, for example, makes for easy access. This is a huge benefit and the opportunity to get into the fresh air is exploited to the full.

There are no class distinctions based on birth and inheritance rights as there are in the UK, although there is the inevitable rich and poor divide that creates some social barriers. In our experience, almost every New Zealander we have met can be accurately described as friendly, considerate and helpful. There is a general dislike of formality, and people tend to see each other as equals, although those in positions of authority are normally referred to by their title: Doctor Smith for example.

Socialising

New Zealanders have very similar social values and way of life to most Western countries, but with some special features. Neighbours and friends think nothing of calling in totally uninvited, as this is considered socially acceptable. A short while after moving into our first home, we were invited into our neighbour's house for drinks and small eats. However, all the immediate neighbours were also invited by our hosts so that we could meet them for the first time in a relaxed, social environment; an extremely thoughtful gesture of welcome and friendliness.

When accepting an invitation somewhere, it is normal to ask the host or hostess what you should bring. The standard reply might be to 'bring a plate', which means a plate of food and not just something to eat off! If they say they are planning to barbecue then don't be afraid to ask what meat to bring. They may ask you to bring a cheese board or dessert instead so be prepared to put together something unexpected. What isn't done in New Zealand is for a guest to turn up with an extremely cheap bottle of fizzy plonk and then proceed to drink the premium beer and quality wine. I can certainly remember that happening at more than one social gathering that we held in the UK! The cornerstone of the social circuit in New Zealand is about sharing and it works very well indeed.

New Zealand *v* Australia

There seemed to be a general perception in the UK that everyone who comes from 'down-under' talks the same and is tarred with the same brush. This could not be further from the truth, although the rivalry that exists between New Zealand and Australia is legendary, and both populations take great delight in telling jokes about each other whether they be politically correct or not. In fact, the more un-politically correct they are, the better!

Sporting encounters between the two countries are considered as almost a matter of life or death in the eyes of many, especially on the rugby field. There is a saying that the Kiwis will support the All Blacks or anyone playing the Australians, which was certainly true during the 2003 Rugby World Cup Final. The Kiwi support for England was quite surreal, but understandable given that a third Australian success would never be lived down on the New Zealand side of the Tasman Sea. Having said that, a recent census determined that about 80 per cent of New Zealanders are of European – mainly British – descent so perhaps it is in the blood! However, it doesn't matter how many games the All Blacks lose, they are still considered to be the best team in the world by their supporters, who will go to great lengths to back up what could be considered a somewhat myopic view at times.

A modern country

A common misconception of New Zealand is that the country is years behind the rest of the modern world because of its geographical remoteness. Friends and family in the UK who knew a friend of a friend who had visited the country were quick to offer advice before we left, such as the shops being closed on Saturday, that you could not buy alcohol on Sunday and that fashion was still in the 70s. How wrong they all were. At one time it certainly was like that, but the country has moved with the times and there is not a great deal of difference from the ways of the UK. That is why it was easy for us to integrate into the lifestyle in such a short period of time.

Shopping

Shopping is a surprisingly pleasant affair as most of the main centres are not particularly overcrowded – with the probable exception of Auckland and anywhere at Christmas of course – and very well laid out. Good quality clothing and designer label stores, together with a wide range of shops, galleries and markets stocking many goods that are simply not available outside the country, are abundant. There is a strong connection with Asia and Japan in particular, that ensures electronic goods such as TVs and cameras are all competitively priced. Good, old-fashioned bartering is very much alive and well, especially where payment by cash is involved. Department stores can be found in every main city, most of which can be compared in both layout and format to the likes of Dingles or Debenhams in the UK, although there seem to be more departments and a greater range of goods on offer under one roof.

Most supermarkets are open seven days a week from 7am to 11pm. The one major difference to similar stores in the UK is that they are only licensed to sell beer and wine: spirits are only available from a liquor or 'bottle' store which also stocks a wide range of wines, beers and mixers.

Dairies are the equivalent of the local corner shop and are located in just about every residential area throughout the country. Many stay open to late in the evening and stock a fairly typical range of household goods, groceries, newspapers, magazines and tobacco products.

FACTS AND FIGURES

- Three million inhabitants on the North Island

- One million inhabitants on the South Island

- Flight times from:

London to Los Angeles	10 hours
Los Angeles to Auckland	12 hours
Auckland to Wellington	1 hour
Wellington to Sydney	3 hours

- Male life expectancy   75.5 years

- Female life expectancy   81.6 years

- Exports: $15.86 billion (£5.9 billion)

- Imports: $16.06 billion (£6.1 billion)

- Time zone: GMT plus 12 hours
  (daylight saving time + or – 1 hour)

- Seasons:

NZ	UK
Spring	Autumn
Summer	Winter
Autumn	Spring
Winter	Summer

- The road distance between Auckland and Wellington is only 658 km but takes eight or more hours to drive.

- There are more than 2,000 indigenous plant species in New Zealand, 1,500 of which are unique to this country.

- The water *does* 'swirl' in the opposite direction to that in UK as it goes down the plughole!

2
Why Emigrate?

'Why emigrate?' is probably the single most significant and challenging question to be addressed.

Friends and family alike will ask why on earth you are even thinking of giving up everything to go and live in New Zealand, although others will be very envious that you have the opportunity or even the courage to do so. Your answer to 'why emigrate?' will be based on a series of factors that helped you to arrive at your own decision to go. It needs to be as convincing to them as it was to you for fear of someone talking you out of it!

WHAT FACTORS?

Every individual will have their own reasons for wanting to leave the UK, but the four factors that always seemed to crop up in conversation during our deliberations were:

- quality of life

- taxation

- job satisfaction

- politics.

It is perhaps worth taking each of these as a separate heading and sharing some experiences that may feature in your own decision-making process.

QUALITY OF LIFE

Quality of life is essentially the most important factor of them all and will feature at the centre of your conversations with family and friends alike. You must be totally self-critical in order to determine what your quality of life is now and how it *will* improve should you achieve immigration to New Zealand. Note that I say how it will improve, because you would not be considering moving if emigration resulted in a lower quality of life than what you have now!

It is extremely difficult to comprehend how a country actually looks and feels without physically going there, something you may have experienced when stepping off a plane for the first time in a foreign land. Having said that, we emigrated to New Zealand without having ever visited the country before in our lives.

There were of course other factors involved, the most prominent being that our move was being 'bonded' by my employer so our financial contribution was minimal in relation to the overall cost of the whole package. I also knew that my initial contract of work was guaranteed for three years and eight months, so income was not at risk barring personal mishap. Overall, we found ourselves in a very attractive position that could not be ignored and merited further investigation.

So what about quality of life? The wide-open spaces, friendly people, relaxed pace of everyday living and clean air are all features of New Zealand that we have very quickly grown to appreciate. We had read about such attributes during the research phase of our journey and it dawned on us that these were the very elements being slowly eroded and undermined in the UK. With no indication that things were going to get any better the decision was virtually made for us. The opportunity to get away from the seven days a week grind that was necessary for comfortable survival in the UK was simply too good to miss.

Family issues

However, the overwhelming desire to move on was tempered by family issues that had to be discussed and addressed. The thought of physically leaving behind family and loved ones will undoubtedly play a part in your initial deliberations and some cope with it better than others. No words in a book can ever hope to guide you in making the ultimate decision to emigrate; your situation is unique but, at some stage, you will have to face up to the reality of exactly how this move will affect everyone you will be leaving behind in the UK.

There will be talk of regular visits back to the UK should your planned move to New Zealand actually come to be a reality. However, while the intention may well be good, the financial implications of flying a family backward and forward will have a very real impact on that notion. A family of four will have to find somewhere in the region of £4,000 for flights and associated departure taxes alone. Add to that the cost of travel in the UK and spending money, and the total funds required would almost certainly exceed what may have been first anticipated or is even affordable. You are strongly advised not to use promises of such trips as bargaining tools for younger children, or to reach a compromise with other family members in order to secure your emigration dream, as there is a very real potential for reneging on the deal!

TAXATION

Everyone has an opinion on how they are taxed and the subject of taxation overseas cropped up early in our deliberations. The tax laws in New Zealand are certainly different from those in the UK and you cannot be recommended strongly enough to do further research on your own situation and potential tax liability.

There are certain tax codes and allowances in New Zealand that function in a similar way to the UK, but they are less clear cut. Everyone who earns an income pays tax, although some workers in certain circumstances can be refunded a portion of the contribution at the end of the financial year.

The budget announced on 22 May 2008 has introduced some wide-ranging changes to personal tax packages with the introduction of a $10.6 billion programme of tax cuts which take effect from 1 October 2008, with further changes scheduled from 1 April 2010 and 2011.

The levels of taxation – using NZ dollars (the exchange rate in this book is assumed to be $2.65 to £1 sterling) – are as follows:

To 30 Sept 2008	From 1 Oct 2008	From 1 Apr 2010	From 1 Apr 2011
15% to $9,500	12.5% to $14,000	12.5% to $17,500	12.5% to $20,000
21% to $38,000	21% to $40,000	21% to $40,000	21% to $42,500
33% to $60,000	33% to $70,000	33% to $75,000	33% to $80,000
39% over $60,000	39% over $70,000	39% over $75,000	39% over $80,000

This is how the amount of tax due to 30 September 2008 (rounded down) on a gross income of $45,000 is then calculated:

$0 to $9,500 @ 15%	= $1,425
$9,501 to $38,000 @ 21%	= $5,984
$38,001 to $45,000 @ 33%	= $2,309
Total	= $9,718

The same calculation applied from 1 Oct 2008 will work as follows:

$0 to $14,000 @ 12.5%	= $1,750
$14,001 to $40,000 @ 21%	= $5,459
$40,001 to $45,000 @ 33%	= $1,649
Total	= $8,858

The following table shows the weekly after-tax take-home increases above the current levels for all three milestones until 2011. The final column indicates the difference in annual tax benefits from the tax arrangements in place prior to 1 Oct 2008.

pre-Oct 2008 ($)	1 Oct 2008 ($)	1 Apr 2010 ($)	1 Apr 2011 ($)	Annual Increase ($)
20,000	12	18	22	1,130
30,000	12	18	22	1,130
40,000	16	22	26	1,370
50,000	16	22	32	1,670
60,000	16	22	32	1,670
70,000	28	34	44	2,270
80,000+	28	39	55	2,870

There is also an automatic deduction made from most types of earnings for Employers Accident Compensation Corporation (ACC). This is a type of 'no fault' insurance to cover the cost of accidental injuries, and applies to all New Zealanders and visitors to New Zealand. The main income exceptions where an ACC levy is not collected are:

- redundancy

- retirement

- some pension funds.

The rate of this levy is generally set at 1.2 per cent for every $100 earned depending on the type of business conducted, so in the example above a further $540 would be deducted.

The level of Government Sales Tax (equivalent to VAT) is set at 12.5 per cent. So on balance taxation levels overall are much the same, although wages can be equated to about half – or less in some cases – that of similar employment in the UK.

Worldwide Income

What should be made absolutely clear is that once you emigrate to New Zealand you are classed as a resident for tax purposes and if you have any other worldwide income then you are required to declare it. This includes any pension payments or investment dividends.

There is a double taxation agreement between the UK and New Zealand, which basically means both countries cannot have full taxation rights on income from other sources, unless you have waived taxation rights in the UK. If you were drawing a pension from UK sources, for example, that amount is converted to dollars by the IRD (Inland Revenue Department) in New Zealand and added to your gross income from your employment in their country. However, if the amount drawn is not taxed in the UK, it certainly will be in New Zealand, so on that basis let's take the previous example showing the figures from 1 Oct 2008 a stage further.

Total pension drawn in the UK is $12,000 per year, which when converted back to sterling amounts to about £4,500. This is below the level at which tax is payable in the UK so the full amount is added onto your wages in New Zealand:

Income = $45,000 per year plus $12,000 pension

Total   = $57,000

$0 to $14,000 @ 12.5%   = $1,750

$14,001 to $40,000 @ 21%   = $5,459

$40,001 to $57,000 @ 33%   = $5,609

    Total   = $12,818

You are entitled to a UK tax code, normally the basic level such as 647L, despite being resident in New Zealand for tax purposes, but this code applies to UK income only – it is not recognised in New Zealand.

There are other benefits attached to this package that affect families with younger children who will gain under the Working for Families policy – similar to UK child benefit as I remember it. An example is a couple with two children under 13 with a joint income of $65,000 per annum will find themselves $42.76 per week better off from 1 Oct 2008, rising to $84.55 per week by 1 Apr 2011.

No matter where you go in the world taxation is always an emotive subject and doing the necessary homework to determine just what your own personal tax levels will be is extremely important to ensure no nasty surprises await you after arriving in the country.

JOB SATISFACTION

How do you measure job satisfaction? Could it be simply stated as enjoyment of your job, or lack of it, or does it go deeper than that? Work is a necessity to survive but just how much does your job impinge on your private life?

We all strive to maintain a comfortable lifestyle and suitable reward for hard work is important. However, having to work six days a week and then attend to household tasks on the seventh day to maintain that chosen lifestyle cannot possibly be regarded as ideal.

Yes, you may be satisfied with your job, but just about anybody would take the opportunity to work five days a week or fewer rather than six, yet still maintain the lifestyle to which they have been accustomed. How much work you commit to is a personal matter but we have realised that there is more opportunity to relax and enjoy leisure time in New Zealand than there ever was in the UK. The exchange rate between the pound and the NZ dollar certainly helps money go further after arrival in New Zealand, so with careful budgeting there is the potential for putting away some funds for future use. However, any tendency to spend, spend, spend on arrival should be resisted as the dollars tend to run out very quickly!

Whilst on the subject of potential earnings, it may be useful to give you a general idea of income before tax in some of the industry sectors in New Zealand, as it may well influence your decision to emigrate or not. The figures in Figure 4 reflect an average of what could be earned within a particular sector, but should not be taken as definitive.

Industry	Number employed	Average salary (before tax)
Building	150,000	£11–23K
Manufacturing	280,000	£11–21K
Education	150,000	£15–26K
Trading (retail and wholesale)	400,000	£10–18K
Hospitality	55,000	£8–13K
Business and financial service	260,000	£13–37K+
Health and community	175,000	£11–37K+
Transport and communications	120,000	£11–30K

Fig. 4. New Zealand incomes.

POLITICS

Everyone has their own political opinion or view and I have no intention of devoting much space to exactly what concerned us the most, but there were certainly some factors that helped swing our decision to go. The incessant tax increases and impositions on property, insurance, wages, fuel, utilities, etc., etc., were costing us more and more each year. The end result was the necessity to work even harder just to meet increasing demands while still trying to maintain a comfortable lifestyle. The UK government continued to assure us that services were improving across the board. Like many millions in the country, we failed to see it that way at all and there was no real benefit evident to us despite tedious and repetitive talk of prudence within the economy. It was definitely time to go and seek a new life elsewhere.

MAKING THE DECISION

No one can make the decision to set out on the emigration trail but you. It would be reasonable to assume that you are reading this book because you harbour a desire to leave the UK and are seriously contemplating living in New Zealand, but there is much, much more to consider. It is wise to suggest that should you be considering emigration as a means of escaping a financial nightmare and starting afresh overseas, you could well be disappointed. It will cost you money that can be ill afforded in a quest that could fail at any stage, and your financial situation can and probably will get even worse.

Emigration cannot and must not be viewed in isolation as a possible solution to a problem. Realistically it is an absolute change of lifestyle and culture, so the decision is not a straightforward one. Although it would be very easy to stop the whole process at any stage and forfeit everything that may have been achieved thus far, the reality is that you would be very reluctant to do so because that would be admitting defeat.

CULTURE SHOCK

Everyone who moves overseas will almost certainly experience some form of culture shock and it is only the level of intensity that varies. Culture shock cannot be explained in terms of one specific characteristic, although it can be illustrated as a form of anxiety about many things. The main symptoms include:

- anger
- resentment
- insomnia
- loneliness
- sadness

- lack of confidence

- difficulty adapting to new cultures

- feelings of vulnerability.

Your experience of culture shock could be affected by other factors such as being single, or migrating as a family where the age of children may have an effect. I suppose that arriving in New Zealand could be related to the joy and excitement of experiencing anything new. This initial experience is commonly referred to as the 'honeymoon period' and I surely don't have to explain the link! However, like a real honeymoon, the fun has to come to an end at some stage and the real work of settling into your new life begins in earnest, whilst the novelty of living in an entirely different environment starts to wear off.

There are many ways to combat culture shock and one of the best is to do something that you have been putting off for years in the UK. Join a club, start a fitness campaign, get out and enjoy the outside life that is so much a part of New Zealand's culture. Nobody can predict the level of culture shock that may affect you or your family – it may be absolutely nothing – but at least you can talk about the issues before you leave the UK and have some sort of preparedness before it jumps out and bites you!

The decision to leave the UK will have already changed your mindset. Unless there are some major obstacles that may prevent you leaving, it is very likely that you will do everything in your power to make sure your plan succeeds.

3

Visa Application

WHAT JOB?

The desire for a different life is the key factor that drives people to pack up and travel to new places and destinations, including New Zealand. However, there is a lengthy procedure to endure and complete before gaining that all-important visa for the opportunity to make the country your permanent home. This chapter provides an insight into what should be addressed at least as a minimum in your decision-making process.

New Zealand has an active immigration policy designed to attract people who value its culture, the country and way of life and are also capable of contributing effectively to the economy. There is a very good level of employment in the country, although that is somewhat countered by a steep decline in the birth rate, resulting in an ageing workforce with fewer young people to replace them. In view of that, immigration requirements are frequently reviewed in order to suit the constantly changing needs of the country and thus maintain its economic prosperity without detriment to the existing workforce.

Businesses in New Zealand are typically small compared with the UK, but there is a wide range of international companies which have established offices and outlets throughout the country. The job market differs from one region to another – for example most government type jobs will be found in and around the capital of Wellington where Parliament and associated ministries are based. Some key trends in the working culture of New Zealand are as follows:

- Mobile phone and computer technology advances mean that work can easily encroach on personal time.

- More people work outside normal business hours because the type of work demands it.

- The number of families earning a dual income has increased significantly over recent years.

- There are more women and single parents in the workforce pro-rata compared with other developed countries.

- Both employers and employees recognise the need to actively balance work and home life.

As already mentioned, quality of life will almost certainly be the key issue on the agenda of any prospective migrant during the quest to secure an interesting job, pleasant working conditions and an attractive salary. The number of people with specific skills in some industries are reported as being at their lowest level for 25 years. On that basis the country will actively seek to recruit the right people from overseas to fill jobs that cannot be routinely covered by those available within the national workforce.

A book we read during our initial research told the story of a couple who emigrated to New Zealand but returned to England four years later. The expectation that the husband's skill in designing luxury yachts for a sea-loving nation would be in big demand was never realised, but the overall theme of the book seemed to be one of hindsight with a message throughout of 'if only'. We were left with a clear impression that this couple simply did not do enough research before they left the UK, and the story is a vivid example of an ambition that was probably doomed to fail from the outset.

Prospective immigrants should be under no illusion that submitting an application for a visa accompanied by a job offer to 'flip burgers' in a world famous fast-food outlet will ever make it past the assessment stage. Such an application will be a complete waste of time and money.

There are enough school leavers and part-time workers from within the country to cover these types of jobs so the New Zealand Immigration Service (NZIS) will target only those people with specific skills to fill a particular niche in the employment market as listed in the Immediate and Long Term Skill Shortage lists. These comprehensive lists have replaced the Priority Occupations List (POL) that operated for many years. They provide details of particular qualifications together with geographical areas with specific vacancies in that trade. See Chapter 10 for more details.

The general wording of such vacancies will appear along the lines of the following examples:

Chef

National Certificate in Cookery at Level 4 and a minimum of five years' combined experience in establishments offering *à la carte*, buffet/banqueting or commercial catering, with a minimum of two years at *chef de partie* (section leader) level or higher. Vacancies exist across all regions of both the North and South Islands.

These qualifications are *mandatory*: definitely no flipping burgers!

Butcher

National Certificate in Level 4 meat retailing (curing, smoking and small goods, carcass boning and forecasting, planning and production). Vacancies in the far South of the South Island only.

Some extensive research on your part is required and you must take an extremely critical look at exactly how you consider your specific skills will be of benefit to the country. Raising any paperwork and committing money in the expectation that an application for a visa will be successful without such research is a recipe for failure. So if you are a luxury yacht builder find out exactly which yard is creaming off the orders, whether there is a viable market future for the product and most importantly, whether there are any vacancies.

The rise in interest rates during our initial years in New Zealand meant that some businesses had been forced to streamline their operations. The recent global recession has seen this trend continue but, perhaps, on a greater scale, if only to protect their future productivity. It is in your best interest to uncover as much information about the long-term viability of a potential employer as soon as practicable.

Unless you have an offer of work with a guaranteed contract it may be seriously worth considering visiting the country. Meeting potential employers face-to-face has always been the best way of both assessing the possibilities and selling your abilities. However, it stands to reason that you would have to be fairly confident even at this early stage of gaining a visa, as such a trip will eat into your available budget and there is still no guarantee of success.

SKILLED/BUSINESS STREAM

The purpose of this stream is to help talented and entrepreneurial migrants gain residency in New Zealand. The largest number of immigration places available in any single year is in this stream. The categories are:

- Skilled Migrant

- Residence from Work

- Business.

This next section focuses on the first of these two categories as they have the highest number of applicants and are more likely to be applicable to readers of this book. Business categories are a specialist area in their own right and never merited further investigation in our own particular situation, but they may yet play a part in your case.

Skilled Migrant Category

There is a well-defined procedure that any prospective migrant must follow to ascertain whether the current level of qualification has been achieved. The starting point is completion of the *Quick Check* to see if the minimum criteria can be met, followed by working through the *Skilled Migrant Category Points Indicator* form. Its sole purpose is for an individual to get an indication of whether they would qualify for the requisite amount of points needed to submit an *Expression of Interest* (EOI) in applying for residence in New Zealand. On receipt of the EOI New Zealand Immigration Service (NZIS) staff will assess the final points score.

The minimum number of points required is constantly under review by the NZIS to ensure that there is a steady flow of applications, so the points level can go up or down depending on economic needs and demands. There have been quite dramatic changes in the requirement over the years, with a high of 180 points being reduced to as low as 100 points, sometimes within a matter of days. The reason for these significant swings is largely the small percentage of applicants qualifying for the higher points level, resulting in a huge downturn of numbers meeting government immigration targets.

It is only after the EOI has been processed, and all the criteria are met in qualifying for enough points, that the NZIS may send an *Invitation to Apply for Residence*.

The process is as follows:

Step 1 Complete an initial self-assessment using the *Skilled Migrant*

Quick Check and *Points Indicator* to determine if you are eligible to submit an *Expression of Interest*.

Step 2   Submit an *Expression of Interest* if the minimum number of points required at the time is achieved. The fee at this stage is about £150 if submission is made online using credit card payment. Submission using a paper form will cost about £190.

Step 3   All EOIs submitted over a number of weeks will be pooled and ranked from highest to lowest points; it is not a case of first come first served. The NZIS will rank EOIs in terms of points claimed and set a selection point. Those with points equal to or exceeding the selection point *may* be invited to apply for residence.

If not selected in the first trawl, the EOI will remain in the pool for a further three months and, if still not selected, will be withdrawn. There is no barrier to submitting a further EOI but a further fee will be payable.

Step 4   Once an official invitation to apply for residence has been received, submission of all other necessary documents to support the claims made in your EOI will be required. This will include medical and police certificates, together with other supporting material requested by NZIS.

Step 5   The NZIS will then look very closely at the applicant's ability to settle successfully and make a real contribution to New Zealand's social and economic development. Verification of information stated in the EOI, medical and police certificates will also be sought as necessary. The outcome of this will be one of the following.

   Approval of the application and the granting of a residence visa or permit.

■ The granting of a temporary work visa or permit which will enable the applicant to settle into skilled employment prior to gaining residence.

■ The application may be declined.

At this stage there should be no doubt that this process is going to cost money, which is not necessarily refundable if the application is eventually declined.

Of all the EOIs submitted, there is an average success rate of around 65 per cent where the applicant is invited to apply for residence. The remainder are returned to the pool, declined or withdrawn by the applicant.

Residence from Work Category

This is a relatively new category that was introduced in 2003 to accommodate an offer of work from a New Zealand employer who is unable to find suitably skilled New Zealanders in the native workforce. This visa is effectively a step towards residence, but other issues may affect your decision to proceed down this route.

Employers who are pre-approved by the NZIS are known as *Accredited Employers*, which means that they do not have to seek approval from the NZIS to recruit from overseas. Should an offer of employment be made from an Accredited Employer you can apply for a visa under the *Talent (Accredited Employers) Work Residence Policy*.

There is one major difference from the Skilled Migrant Category in that no points are required, but other criteria to meet eligibility are:

■ Applicants must have a genuine job offer from an accredited employer in New Zealand that pays an annual base salary of $55,000.

■ Applicants must be under the age of 55.

■ The offer of employment must be on a full-time basis for a minimum of two years and in the employer's main business activity where they are directly responsible for your output.

- Once your visa has been approved, you may only work for an accredited employer for the duration of the visa.

- Application for residence can only be made after two years of living and working in New Zealand.

This visa is a multiple entry work permit that states the exact work you are permitted to undertake whilst in the country and is valid for 30 months. The additional six months over and above the 24 months required for residency qualification is designed to allow time for your residency application to work through the system. However, there are some potential problems with this projected timeline that must not be ignored.

On average, an application for residency will take anywhere from six to 12 months to process and the 24-month qualifying period required before an application can be submitted to the NZIS actually starts from the date that you arrive in the country. The timing of your application under this visa is a bit like the chicken and egg conundrum. You will not want to go any further with your plans to emigrate until your visa has been actually granted. However, the 30-month validity of the visa is counted from the day of issue and not the day you actually arrive in New Zealand. We set foot in the country nearly three months after the issue date of the visa, which effectively means that there will only be three months spare once qualified for residency to actually be granted that status.

The potential to not have gained residency when your visa expires is very real and you must ensure that the NZIS is aware of your circumstances should this situation arise in your case.

You will need to submit further medical and police certificates with your application for residency in order to meet the timelines stipulated by the NZIS. More on these requirements can be found in the following sections of this chapter.

Sponsorship under the Talent (Arts, Culture and Sports) Residence Policy is another option that falls largely under the same rules as the Accredited policy. Other types of visa that could be investigated are listed under the family, business and entrepreneur categories – the rules for each are very different. Statistics show that Accredited and Talent are the categories under which the majority of applicants apply. Of the 30,000 or so people who will be approved as part of a typical year's immigration programme, up to 22,000 will be under the Skilled Migrant Category with the remainder coming from Work to Residence, Investor, Entrepreneur and employees of relocating business categories.

Business Category

As one might expect, there are some very different conditions to be fulfilled if you are planning to arrive in New Zealand and set up a business. The requirements for good health and character are no different from other visas, but you must also submit a sound business plan and provide evidence that you have enough capital to start up your intended business. In addition, there must be enough separate funds to support you, your partner and children if applicable.

Providing you meet all the necessary criteria, the NZIS will grant you a work permit initially valid for nine months. It may not seem long, but you can then apply for a further permit that will take your total stay up to three years. In order to achieve this, you will need to prove that you are making reasonable progress in your business venture through audited accounts, tax records, property documents, invoices and other general information from sources such as banks, utility companies and the local council.

An acceptable business plan will need to show details of realistic financial forecasts, relevant experience, no business failures in the previous five years and certainly no fraudulent or underhand dealings! More importantly, you will need to convince the NZIS that your proposed business venture will be of benefit to New Zealand. Remember the 'flipping burgers' statement earlier? Setting out to open a fast-food outlet is probably not what the country is looking for – there are plenty already.

There are also different rules regarding Occupational Registration in New Zealand. A good example is a hair salon in the UK that wants to carry out ear piercing, and has to undergo an inspection and gain a certificate from their local council before they can make that part of their operation, although there are no similar checks for the hairdressing part of the business itself. In New Zealand there is no requirement to register an individual in a hair salon to carry out ear piercing, but the salon owner must register the salon for the purpose of carrying out hairdressing. There must be many other examples like this that will need thorough research in order to ensure that a proposed venture does not fall foul of the law.

Funds are critical to establishing a sound business, and the NZIS will be looking for sufficient collateral sources such as in a New Zealand bank account, recognised credit cards with a healthy level of funds available and travellers' cheques. The business category has been designed specifically to attract long-term investors to the country and accordingly, the bar has to be set very high.

BIRTH CERTIFICATES

You are required to submit a full birth certificate with your visa application. I was totally unaware that such a thing existed, and we did not possess them so an application had to be submitted to the various registrars in the places of birth for each member of the family listed in the application. A full birth certificate is printed on A4 size paper and is very much more detailed than the standard 'small' version.

Details of your local registrar can be found in the telephone directory and they in turn will be able to provide full contact details of every registrar in the country, together with the required application forms. The cost of this at the time was £7 per certificate and as all the applicants for our visas were all born in districts administered by different authorities, it required four separate applications and associated payments. Details can be found at www.gro.gov.uk.

POLICE CERTIFICATES

This is not as sinister as it sounds unless of course an applicant has a police record! It is a requirement of the NZIS that in order to grant a visa they need to be sure that the applicant *and* all family members over the age of 17 included on the visa application are of good character. This requirement is to ensure that the general interests and security of New Zealanders will not be put at risk.

In general, the NZIS will not grant a visa or permit if you:

- Have ever been convicted and sentenced to a prison term of five years or more.

- Have been convicted and sentenced to a prison term of 12 months or more in the past ten years.

- Have ever been deported from New Zealand or any other country.

- Are believed to be associated with criminal or terrorist groups or are in some way a perceived danger to New Zealand.

Other offences connected with immigration, drugs and violence will almost certainly result in an application being denied.

Police certificates are issued by ACRO (Association of Chief Police Officers Criminal Records Office). There are two services available – standard and fast track, designed for those wishing to obtain a visa quickly. The processing time from receipt to dispatch of the certificate is ten and two working days respectively. The standard fee is £35 and the fast track fee is £70. You can find all the details on the ACPO website at www.acpo.police.uk/certificates.asp.

A police certificate must be no more than six months old at the time an application is lodged. If any certificate(s) become a year old from date of issue before a decision on an application is made, then be prepared for the possibility of producing further police certificate(s) if the NZIS requires it.

Proof of identity must be submitted with the application and must be original documentation. It will be returned with your certificate(s) once processed.

MEDICAL CERTIFICATES

Completing the medical and chest x-ray requirements for submission with the visa application is liable to be the most expensive part of the process. The NZIS maintains a list of approved Panel Doctors and Radiologists in the UK who are the only ones authorised to conduct medical examinations for emigration purposes. The full list of approved doctors appears on the NZIS website.

Although the nearest, most convenient doctor to us was a private practice – the fees were accordingly extortionate – that might not be the case in your area and it could be worth shopping around. The total cost of gaining medical certificates for our visa exceeded £700 and, as was highlighted earlier, there is no guarantee of being granted a visa even if you are medically fit.

Residency applications must be able to meet each of the following criteria in all cases:

- Unlikely to be a danger to public health.

- Unlikely to impose significant cost or demands on New Zealand's health services and/or education services.

- Able to undertake the functions for which you were granted entry.

Chest x-rays will be required for every applicant aged 11 years and over, but pregnant women are exempt.

There is a list of medical conditions that are considered by the New Zealand health authorities to be significantly costly to treat, or for which treatment may be in high demand. If any applicant is unfortunate enough to suffer one of these conditions, they will be considered not to have met an acceptable standard of health for residency purposes unless granted a medical waiver.

However, if an applicant has severe haemophilia, conditions requiring renal dialysis or active TB then a medical waiver will not be granted.

The timely completion of all required medicals is more crucial than obtaining police certificates, as they must be no more than three months old at the time of lodging the visa application. Careful planning for this part of the process is paramount. Full details of health requirements are contained on the NZIS website.

If a visa has been issued under the Residence to Work Policy, residency is not granted until at least 24 months have been spent in the country. You are required to provide the NZIS with another full medical and x-ray certificate, and further police certificate, at your own expense. This is because the original checks that were completed at the time of application for the visa are deemed to be out of date for the purpose of any residency application.

PASSPORTS

Every applicant, including children, must be in possession of their own up-to-date passport which will need to cover the whole period of the travel visa as a minimum. It is worth considering renewing passports before leaving the UK, if only to ensure that you do not have to worry about it for another ten years unless you elect to become a citizen of New Zealand, after which you will be eligible to apply for a New Zealand passport. The current minimum time that must be spent in New Zealand to qualify for citizenship is 240 days in every year, for five consecutive years from the date that permanent residency was granted. Potentially, it could be seven years before you are entitled to hold a New Zealand passport so maintaining your British passport is essential.

The cost of renewing a single British passport through the British High Commission in Wellington has recently been reviewed and fees are charged as follows:

- 32-page adult passport for a person 16 years or over
  (valid 10 years) £120

- 32-page child passport for a person under 16 (valid 5 years) £76

- 48-page adult passport (valid 10 years) £145

I have no idea why the charges are so much more than in the UK when the passport you are issued is identical, but it is nevertheless an unnecessary cost that could well be avoided with some careful planning.

SUMMARY

There is a great deal of information to absorb, consider and even discard during the visa process. It cannot be recommended strongly enough that professional advice be sought if there is any doubt over any aspect. There are specialist advisors who will offer their expertise and review immigration plans on your behalf, but be prepared to pay for the service and be very aware that nobody is able to guarantee you gaining that all-important visa. However, advisors will certainly be able to cover all angles to ensure you get the best possible chance of success.

Internet research is by far the quickest and cheapest way to gain the information needed. If you are not already into using the web then you will be staggered at the quantity and depth of information that can be uncovered via a home computer with internet access. As stated in the preface, rules and regulations are subject to regular change. The NZIS website will provide you with all the up-to-date information you need about visas: www.immigration.govt.nz.

The approximate cost for an average family of four to even get to the visa application stage will almost certainly exceed £1,000 but only if the process is completed without the help of an emigration consultant. Fees for medical and police certificates will not be returned to you if your visa is refused.

Prospective applicants must be prepared to write off this sort of money if a bid is not successful. The commitment to spending of this magnitude, with the possibility of nil return, will be a measure of just how determined a potential immigrant is to leave the UK for a new life in New Zealand. The importance of research is once again the key to success and, if there is little chance of gaining a visa from the outset, submitting an application in the desperate hope that it may become a reality is a very risky approach.

4

Emigration Preparations

This is the largest and most detailed chapter in the book because it attempts to cover virtually every facet of preparation for moving you, your family and all your worldly possessions to the other side of the planet.

Be in no doubt that this whole procedure takes considerable effort and patience, so remember the old but wise saying – Rome wasn't built in a day! As we mentioned earlier, *nobody said this was going to be easy* neatly summed up everything in the six months prior to leaving in a few simple words.

SPIDERGRAM

Everyone will have their own way of tackling the biggest move of their life and this method is merely one option that we made use of in preparing for that move. Creating a spidergram is nothing new and is used for planning purposes, primarily in business circles, across the world. It is simply a way of graphically illustrating on paper all the thoughts, ideas and actions that emerge from verbally working through a task or challenge – an excellent way of approaching the whole emigration process.

A simple example of a spidergram given overleaf is to show the steps needed to make a cup of tea. In your mind, every action needed to produce the end result can be visualised to make a graphic illustration of how to do it. This may be an extremely basic procedure, but it conveys all the essential parts of a task as an easy to follow set of instructions. It is this sort of process that can be applied to just about every task requiring completion before the ultimate goal of emigration can be achieved. The resultant piece of paper is of course going to be huge, which is precisely the reason why a spidergram must be easy to follow.

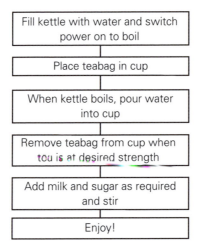

Fig. 5. Sample spidergram.

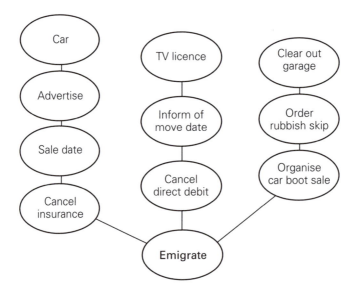

Fig. 6. Emigration spidergram.

Our spidergram (see Fig. 6 opposite) was constructed by using the reverse side of some old wallpaper rolls, and covered a large section of wall in our dining room, an important location as it was visible during mealtimes and could be used as a central point of discussion by the whole family. The illustration in Figure 6 may be of use to get you started.

The plus side of doing things this way was that everyone involved took an interest, and maintained a keen sense of attention to detail and of when something else could be struck off as complete. It also allows children to make their own mark, giving them a sense of purpose, importance and contribution to the process.

SELLING YOUR HOUSE

It is said that buying and selling a house is at the top of the league of stress related activities in life and I can categorically state that there is 100 per cent truth in that statement!

Timing is crucial, and moving out of your house will ideally be tied in with the removal of all furniture and belongings to New Zealand. However, as most people will have no doubt experienced at least once in their life, selling a house by a particular date can never be guaranteed. In a fluctuating housing market this is probably the biggest uncertainty of all.

Our own particular chain of events highlights perfectly how a plan is easily wrecked. We first marketed our property in May and were quietly confident that the house would sell quickly. Our eventual buyer made an offer at the end of September; we emigrated to New Zealand in mid-October and finally completed the house sale in early December.

Nearly seven months to sell the house was certainly not the intended plan, but had we not stuck with our intended timetable to leave the country, the conseqences could have included:

- delay in household belongings shipping date

- not meeting the start date of new job in New Zealand

- lack of insurance cover (cancelled policies)

- rearranging flight bookings (additional fees)

- postponement of farewell party for 150 family and friends (loss of deposits)

- logistics of completing the house sale from the other side of the world (extreme stress!).

Other aspects may well apply in your own situation, but the overall lesson to be learnt from this is that nobody can predict whether a house will take weeks, months or possibly even years to sell. The best advice I would offer is to look closely at the market trends in the area to determine the optimum time for joining the 'for sale' fraternity. Of course this may dent your ambition to emigrate on a particular date, but completing the sale of the house before you leave the UK should be viewed as a positive achievement even if it means moving into rented accommodation temporarily.

Completing all the legal formalities and putting the money raised in the bank will alleviate the worry of some major issues including:

- Setting up power of attorney to complete outstanding paperwork.

- Arranging transfer of proceeds from the sale to your New Zealand bank account.

- Insurance cover for the property (it may be empty but is there any cover for damage prior to completing the sale?).

- Squatters (you never know!).

- Maintenance (blocked gutters, grass cutting, etc.).

- Bill payments.

◼ Additional cost in New Zealand for rented accommodation until funds are received from the sale of your UK house.

Our problem was very much alleviated by a family member offering to act as our agent and, as his own home was literally a few hundred yards down the road, it made our move so much easier.

REMOVAL COMPANY

There is a wide selection of international removal companies located throughout the UK and it would be somewhat biased to recommend any one in particular. However, some aspects should be looked at carefully before contracting a firm to pack and ship your belongings.

Household goods are shipped to New Zealand in a steel container, a journey that takes an average of between six and eleven weeks depending on the route and itinerary of the ship. The cost of this will generally be anywhere from about £2,500 upwards, depending on the cubic capacity of the container used, although there may be some slightly cheaper options through sharing a container with other shippers. Realistically, transfer by sea is the most cost effective way to move your house contents to New Zealand, although there are options for air cargo if you need to do things quickly.

The assessment to determine what size container will be required is completed during the visit of a removal company representative, who will estimate the cubic capacity of the house contents to be moved. It is strongly recommended that estimates from at least three companies are obtained, as all have a different approach, but the eventual decision will be whether to use either an industry-standard 20- or 40-foot container.

The assessor is very competent at estimating what capacity will be required, but some factors need to be considered to ensure the assessment is accurate. Simply instructing the assessor to take everything in a particular area, especially storage spaces such as lofts and under-stair cupboards, is not recommended as this will almost certainly result in transporting items that have no use in New Zealand. Additionally, it will hamper the team who arrive to pack up the house and may well take them extra time to do the job, as they are not being paid to sort your possessions but merely to ensure that they are securely packed for transport in the container. Trying to sort possessions as they are being packed is also a non-starter, as you will end up with everything being packed in a rush and possibly not being ready for the container when it does arrive. Remember, the shipping companies run to a very tight schedule and the sailing of a cargo ship will not be delayed because your container was not at the dockside for loading on time.

Preparing for the move

This is an ideal time to have a complete clear-out of the house and the keyword in this whole operation is ruthlessness. Be absolutely critical when it comes down to deciding what items to take and whether they will be of practical use or no use at all. Some items will not have seen the light of day for years and you may wonder why they have been 'stored' for all this time. It took us almost three months to sort out our house before the assessors arrived, and the single four-ton skip we thought would be ample to dispose of rubbish was needed twice.

Some very useful tips are:

- If you have a 'spare' room, use it to store items that will not be used before emigrating.

- If you have a garage, clear it for storage use.

- Involve the whole family in sorting out the house.

- Do not even think about disposing of sentimental items (especially belonging to children) without full consultation with all concerned.

- Pack items such as photo albums, DVDs, videos and CDs in unsealed boxes.

- Mark boxes clearly and pile 'around' rather than 'in' a room to allow for easy access.

- Do not pack delicate items as this will be done by the shipping company.

- Set aside items for a car boot sale or disposal as appropriate.

- Order the skip at the last possible moment to ensure it will hold the amount of rubbish accumulated.

There are several options for passing on clothes, toys and general items that are no longer of use to you. Everyone will have received donation bags through their door at some stage from charities asking for your unwanted items of clothing. If you have enough to fill more than one bag then take the trouble to ring the organisation and ask them to deliver more sacks to you. They will gratefully collect the filled bags from your house, so the whole exercise is at no cost to you, but will benefit others enormously.

Consider donating unwanted televisions, VCRs and stereo systems to a hospital or an old folks' home if anyone else in your family does not really have a use for them. If you uncover an old games console that is still in working order, but hasn't been used in years, head for the nearest hospital children's ward with it. The appreciation and delight shown by the unfortunate occupants of these places is far more rewarding than simply giving them away to friends and neighbours who will 'take them off your hands' and feel they are doing you a favour.

Packing and moving

The removal company will provide every conceivable type of material required to wrap and pack every last item of your house contents. Larger items of furniture for instance are wrapped in thick, waxed paper that has a thin charcoal layer to prevent sweating, whilst letting the contents breathe. To meet insurance requirements and ensure that everything actually arrives at its destination, a full inventory of items is compiled by the removal company during the packing process. This is why boxes that may have already been filled should not be sealed, as the team will need formally to note the contents and may want to repack some of it anyway.

The removal team will take two or three days to complete the packing of the house, depending on the assessment made some weeks earlier, on what is and is not being taken, and will load the container on the final day. Containers filled with household goods are carried in the hold of a ship and not on the deck where they may be susceptible to extremes of heat and weather on their journey to the Southern Hemisphere. There is no need to worry about dehumidifiers or other devices to protect the contents.

HOUSEHOLD AND ELECTRICAL EQUIPMENT

The New Zealand power system runs at the same voltage as in the UK. There is nothing more to do to most electrical appliances other than to change the plug once they have been unpacked at your destination, although be advised that New Zealand plugs are not fitted with fuses. Sounds straightforward, but there are other issues to be considered when deciding what appliances to take. The most important of these is the servicing and spares support.

Televisions

The transmission frequency of pictures in New Zealand is aligned to those of the UK, so technically any television set you bring with you should receive a picture by connecting an aerial and retuning the set. However, sound transmission is broadcast on a different frequency to that of the UK and the set will need to be adjusted to accommodate this. The manufacturer should be able to verify whether a particular make and model can be adjusted accordingly.

A television set that cannot be modified could still be used as a monitor by connection through a VCR, which has been purchased on arrival in New Zealand, and so will be capable of receiving both sound and pictures. The drawback with this is that you would only be able to record the channel you are actually watching unless there was a second VCR linked to the set.

If the intention is to export a large screen set then check with the removal company about additional charges for the manufacture of a packing crate to safely transport it. Projection TVs, for example, contain a large, highly polished mirror that is very expensive to replace in the event of damage and may be financially prohibitive or even not available as a spare part in New Zealand. The insurance cover for such items is crucial and the removal company will take every measure to ensure that delicate, expensive goods are protected to the highest possible standard.

VCR

From a financial point of view, it is not really worth looking into modifying a VCR even if it was capable of being adjusted, as the cost of a brand new unit in New Zealand is only about £60. Your VCR can still be used to play back videos on any TV, but will not be capable of recording programmes in New Zealand without adjustment. Second-hand VCRs are virtually worthless in the UK, so consider donating them to the local hospital children's ward, school or old folks' home, where they will certainly be actively used and appreciated.

DVD

A DVD player is normally electronically labelled by means of a code for operation within one of six specific geographical world regions. For example, the USA is classed as Region 1 and this means all DVD players sold within the US are coded to Region 1 specifications. The DVD disc is also produced within a specific region, so unless the player code matches the disc code it will be physically impossible to view the film.

According to what the public are told, this is a simple method of protecting copyright and film distribution rights, but making vast profits for the film studio is probably a more realistic ploy. Movies are released in different parts of the world at different times so the summer blockbuster in the US may end up being the Christmas blockbuster somewhere else overseas. If that occurs then the DVD version of the film could already be available to the public in the US while it is being premiered elsewhere. In order to protect the financial integrity of the theatrical distribution of a particular film, the intention was to make it impossible for someone in the US to send a DVD copy of the film to the country where it is in release. Another more believable but unproven theory is the possible price-fixing of DVDs depending on the region.

Manufacturers' 'multi-region' codes are available via the Internet for virtually any DVD player on the market. They will unlock the set and allow the user to view discs from any region. The codes of some models remain guarded by the manufacturer, who will charge a fee to unlock the player at one of their service centres. If the service centre has charged for the job then ask them to demonstrate that it has been unlocked for multi-region use, to ensure that the equipment will work once it has been set up in New Zealand.

Again, service support is an issue that will have to be weighed up, but a new, basic, non-branded DVD player sells for a mere £35 in New Zealand, so it may well not be worth bothering to take one with you. We brought our DVD players with us for use until they failed beyond repair – only one had to be unlocked by a registered dealer before shipping. A new DVD player bought in New Zealand is already unlocked for multi-region use, as there is no law here to say that there should be a tie to any particular region.

Hi-fi and stereo systems

Radio tuners on such systems are universal, so plan to export CD players, radios and other audio equipment if their value makes it worth doing. The price of new equipment in New Zealand is comparable to the UK but, why incur unnecessary expenditure if your UK equipment still has a reasonable life expectancy?

Washing machine

Washing machine hose fittings are generally universal or easily adapted if required, although the availability of spares remains a potential issue. The American-style top loaders appear more popular in New Zealand but there is an ever-increasing range of front loaders coming onto the market. So, if a cheap repair by UK standards is required to an imported front loader, it could cost an inordinate amount of money and time if parts have to be shipped in; check with the UK manufacturer of your machine about service support overseas. Unless the washing machine is virtually brand new, it is worth considering leaving it as part of the fittings with the house, or selling it before leaving the UK. Typically, a good quality machine in New Zealand costs anything from $800 to $1200 and there is certainly plenty of choice.

Tumble dryer

A wall mounted tumble dryer seems to be the most common fitting in New Zealand, so they are adapted for upside-down use with the controls at the bottom, i.e. in easy reach once fixed to the wall. Many houses have a separate laundry room complete with a separate washtub, but there is not always room to fit both washing machine and tumble dryer within the floor space available. The same criteria regarding spares and repair apply to these as to washing machines.

Vacuum cleaner

Dyson is a popular brand in New Zealand, so spares support is very good, but there is also a range of good quality machines that again may not be readily recognised in the UK market and vice versa. Some modern homes have a 'central vac' system, but a stand-alone cleaner is still the only way to vacuum in most cases. To meet import controls, your vacuum cleaner must be spotlessly clean otherwise it could be impounded during the MAF inspection of the container contents on arrival.

Portable electric heaters and radiators

If there is room in the container then have them included in the inventory, as they simply plug into the mains after changing the plug. New Zealand suffers from cold weather during the winter months as well.

Fridges and freezers

The same logic applies as to other appliances – spares and servicing support could be a major factor. If the fridge and freezer are integral to a fitted kitchen in the UK then there is no decision to make, as they will stay as part of the house. We had a small additional chest freezer that was virtually brand new, which in hindsight would have negated the need to buy new in New Zealand. If there is room in the container then ship them, as they are durable items that need no regular servicing. Houses in New Zealand are sold with chattels such as a hob, oven and dishwasher included, but do not normally include fridge, freezer, washing machine or tumble dryer unless specifically listed.

UK extension leads and adaptors

Many small electrical appliances work from a hard-wired transformer unit that plugs directly into the mains and steps the voltage down from 240V to as low as 6V in some cases. These units cannot be plugged directly into the mains system in New Zealand without using a UK–NZ adaptor. Such things as Christmas tree lights and mobile phone chargers spring to mind, so it is worth putting a few UK two or four-way extension lead adaptors in the container so that the UK plug on the end can simply be changed for a New Zealand one on arrival, giving you multiple UK sockets for the price of one New Zealand plug. If the extension board has a fitted fuse then bringing a small supply of spares is advisable to ensure a longer life. Whilst on the subject of Christmas lights, ensure also that a supply of spare lamps is included if you are taking UK sets with you, as it is highly unlikely that you will find a match in New Zealand.

Mobile phones

Very much a personal choice, but modern mobile phones are capable of operating virtually anywhere in the world and you may wish to take 'old faithful' with you. However, in the same way as DVD players are locked to a country, mobile phones are generally locked to a network and may therefore need to be unlocked before leaving the UK. Best advice is to check with the network provider to ascertain the suitability of any phone for operation overseas. The two biggest providers of mobile services in New Zealand are Vodafone and NZ Telecom. Universal-size SIM cards are available for the Vodafone network but NZ Telecom phones are SIM free. A new player in the mobile market is a company called 2° (Two Degrees) and they are proving to be good competition to the 'big two' in terms of new customers having signed up over 15,000 in the first few months of operation. Phones are generally priced much the same as in the UK. There are some very good deals around, such as a monthly fee of $10 (about £3.70) on your account that will give you virtually unlimited text messaging for a year. There have been reported cases where text-mad users have sent over 15,000 messages in a single year, which is a staggering 40 per day every day, and the relative $120 cost per year is extremely favourable compared with how much users in the UK seem to pay.

Garden furniture and equipment

The bio-security regulations for the import of goods into New Zealand are strictly enforced. Virtually everything connected with gardening or the outdoors is carefully inspected, especially goods from the UK following the last foot and mouth epidemic that swept the country. Some of the things that the Ministry of Agriculture and Forestry (MAF) officials will have an interest in with respect to quarantine issues are:

- wooden items

- gardening equipment

- lawn mowers

- cane furniture

- bicycles

- vacuum cleaners

- ornaments and curios containing skin or feathers

- Christmas decorations

- dried flowers and seeds

- equipment used with horses or other animals

- used vehicles.

Sports equipment

Most sports equipment is liable to be inspected by MAF officials when it arrives in the country. This will certainly apply to camping and hiking equipment, and golf clubs are a particular favourite. It is in your interest to ensure they are spotlessly clean prior to the removal company packing them into the container.

An industrial grade disinfectant called Virkon S® is recognised and used by over 40 countries to ensure cleanliness of goods crossing their borders. It was made available to us in spray form by the removal company, although there was an additional charge of £20 for the service. The removal company should indicate on the inventory sheets exactly which items have been cleaned and treated, but this will still not deter MAF inspecting them on arrival in New Zealand if they deem it necessary. There is a strong possibility that they will block entry of those items that have not been treated.

VEHICLES

If you intend to ship a car from the UK to New Zealand, some issues need to be addressed. Your car will be shipped in the same container as domestic goods (almost certainly a 40 foot size) and packed within a wooden frame so as to make maximum use of space around and above it. On arrival in New Zealand it will be subjected to an extremely thorough inspection to ensure there is absolutely no trace of mud or dirt anywhere on the vehicle. There is a story doing the rounds in New Zealand about an imported car that had a leaf trapped in the cable loom under the bonnet. The result was that under bio-security regulations, the whole vehicle had to be steam cleaned at the owner's expense before MAF would release it.

All light vehicles (less than 3,500 kg) entering New Zealand for the first time have to go through a series of checks before they can be used on the road. The process is the same whether the vehicle is imported for sale or private use by the owner and is carried out as follows:

- MAF quarantine inspection (identity check, odometer reading, any significant signs of damage).

- Clear customs, but the vehicle must be transported to an Entry Certifier by trailer or towing as it has yet to be certified as roadworthy.

- Entry certification (registration, licensing and Warrant of Fitness (MOT) testing).

The cost of this process is about £400, but does not include the Goods and Service Tax (GST) of 12½ per cent payable on the value of the vehicle. First time immigrants may be able to import a vehicle without paying GST, providing the customs service is satisfied that they are taking up permanent residence, have owned and used the vehicle for at least one year and agree that they will continue to use the vehicle for at least a further two years.

There are some very good deals to be struck with car showrooms in New Zealand, especially when paying by cash, and there is a huge range of quality used vehicles to choose from. The price of both new and used vehicles in the country is cheaper than in the UK, despite everything having to be imported as no car manufacturing industry exists in New Zealand. Toyota is the market leader, with Ford and Holden (General Motors) sharing second place.

TV LICENCE

The UK television licence can only be renewed in minimum blocks of three months, which may mean that it could become invalid before leaving your house. Ours expired a mere ten days before we left and it was simply not worth the expense to renew it for a further three months. Taking the option to renew it quarterly at about nine months before you plan to emigrate may well be cost effective and convenient, but you will need to talk to the licensing authorities well in advance. We made an assumption that renewing the licence for a month or so would be quite feasible and I jokingly informed the licensing agent that we would just have to take the risk for the ten remaining days in the country. The sinister response was 'we know where you live', so the borrowed TV was returned and we spent the last period of living in the UK enjoying life without it.

No TV licence is required in New Zealand, but the quality of reception can vary dramatically and is generally not as good as in the UK because of the mountainous terrain. Subscription services via satellite and cable are the only alternatives in some areas.

INSURANCES

Insurance policies for almost any situation requiring cover will have an expiry or review date, although cancellation of some appears to be infinitely more difficult than for others. The insurances detailed below are based on our experience only, so it would be wise to expect different results depending on individual company policy. You are strongly advised to ensure that anything you might arrange via telephone, especially when dealing with insurance, is backed up with a letter to the company in order to formally confirm whatever arrangements have been agreed.

Life

It is entirely feasible to continue paying into an existing life policy and still have full cover, although this may require the maintenance of a UK bank account for monthly direct debit premiums. A fairly typical life policy in New Zealand amounts to circa £55 per month for cover of about £100,000 so prices are generally comparable with the UK. Cancellation of any UK based life cover will ideally tie up with the intended travel date to New Zealand, but check with the company if cover extends to worldwide travel, and emigration in particular, as it may be financially in your favour until your journey down under is complete.

Home contents

Once the house has been packed into the container there are unlikely to be any home contents to insure. The removal company provides all insurance cover for goods whilst in transit and to the point of delivery, so your own home contents policy can normally be cancelled at very short notice by a telephone call to your provider. You will know the date that your house is being packed up, so why not pre-empt the cancellation of the policy by notifying the insurance company of the date and approximate time when the container leaves the property on its journey to New Zealand?

Buildings

If you are unfortunate enough to have not sold the house before leaving the UK, it is strongly recommended to investigate what building cover may need to be maintained until the sale is actually completed. A reduced premium may be in order, especially if the house is empty, so check with the policy provider. Otherwise, cover should be easy to cancel.

Endowment

The performance of endowment policies has been the subject of much media attention over the years and our own policy was only one of many thousands affected. A majority of endowment policies bought in the early eighties were sold with unfounded promises in the sales pitch that even a basic £30,000 plan could generate as much as 50 per cent profit at maturity. It was widely recognised that few, if any, would in fact be worth enough to pay off the capital unless a huge injection of cash was made, and the retirement nest-egg dreams of many were entirely dashed.

You are obliged to ask your mortgage provider if they have an interest in the policy, although the answer is liable to be no. This leaves the holder free to do with it what they want, but it is essential to obtain a written declaration from the mortgage provider of their stated position.

The decision to surrender our endowment was eventually taken, but regretfully the delay of two months in going ahead with this resulted in a further £2,300 being lost from its previous value. We elected to treat the funds we raised from this surrender as separate from anything to do with the house sale and they were duly sent to New Zealand for use on arrival to buy vehicles, phones, insurance, etc.

Do remember, however, that the sole basis of the endowment policy was to ensure that sufficient funds were available to at least repay the initial capital borrowed to buy the house, so any money sent to New Zealand before emigration has to be accounted for. Whatever sum is raised by the surrender of such a policy should be offset against the equity raised through the sale of the house, as the mortgage provider will still want their capital back. Treating any such surrender of an endowment as a financial advance of funds is probably the best approach.

> **Warning**
>
> An endowment policy should not be cancelled or surrendered until an immigration visa has been issued by the NZIS as the consequences of doing so could be financially disastrous.

Car

This is easy to cancel by simply telling the company that you will no longer own the vehicle from a particular time and date. If it is left until the last minute before you leave the country, ensure that any refund can be made direct to your bank account or can be handled by someone on your behalf.

Consumer insurance (warranties)

Warranties on electrical equipment in particular are transferable within the UK in some cases, but we didn't find any which would or could consider providing an overseas service. Understandable really given that the warranty was applicable to an appliance that was going to be 12,500 miles away!

However, it is worth enquiring if a particular warranty can be transferred to the new owner of the appliance if the intention is to sell it, as it might increase its sale value. Some warranties offer a full refund of the premium paid in the event that no claims are made over the period of the warranty. It might therefore be financially beneficial to at least enquire about maintaining payments for a couple of months if one is about to expire. However, the likely outcome is that once you have moved abroad or sold the goods, the offer will be declared void. Beware of asking companies to make refunds via a third party as they may refuse to do so as part of an anti-fraud policy.

CREDIT CARDS

Management of credit cards is very much a personal matter, but realistically cancellation and repayment of UK based cards would be better settled before leaving the country. Servicing credit and store card accounts from a distance simply adds to the hassle factor and making payments to them would be difficult unless money was regularly flowing into a UK bank account.

There is a whole range of credit cards on offer in New Zealand and most have incentives as a reward for regular use; some interest rates are as low as 13 per cent. Many people put everything on their credit card during the working month, but pay the balance at the end of that month before interest charges kick in. This is done to collect the reward points or air miles. There are stories of some people who have qualified for multiple return flights to Australia from New Zealand in a single year, effectively costing nothing providing a zero balance is maintained.

LOYALTY CARDS

The UK seems to thrive on loyalty cards as stores and companies compete for a hard-earned share of the market. This is not the case in New Zealand, although there is one national organisation called Fly Buys that is accepted in a range of outlets including some petrol stations and supermarkets.

It is recommended that cancellation of all UK reward cards be completed at an early stage of the emigration plan so that any rewards attached to them can be claimed or cashed in – you will want to pack bulky goods in the container and not your suitcase. Some companies may allow transfer of accumulated points to a nominated person, so this could be another way of cashing in on your years of loyalty. There is usually a freephone contact number on the back of the card that will give you access to the company servicing the scheme.

UTILITY BILLS

It is fairly straightforward to arrange a final reading of gas, electric and water meters as the bills are normally forwarded to the new address for settlement. We arranged for our last bills to be paid through a member of our family, as none of the utility companies in our region appeared to have a policy to forward settlements to a temporary address in New Zealand. There is the option of paying an additional amount in advance and relying on the company to refund any excess to a bank account, but if the intention is to not have a UK account once you have emigrated, this presents a further complication that should be avoided if possible. The utility providers in your region may have a different approach or method of dealing with this; early contact with the customer services department is recommended.

STANDING ORDERS/DIRECT DEBITS

Anyone who runs a bank account will almost certainly have standing orders and direct debits. Cancellation of these at the earliest possible opportunity is highly recommended. If they are connected with goods purchased rather than services provided, ensure you forward a letter to the company requesting confirmation that your balance has been cleared and all personal details are removed from their database. Forwarding of mail from the UK is an option for a set period of time, but the junk mail that will certainly be included if companies of this nature are not informed will be irritating, to put it mildly. A typical example is the unsolicited invitation to borrow vast sums of money, as a 'valued customer' in view of your previous account record with another company and one would assume that the offer is not valid outside the UK anyway. If you do expect mail from the UK and, as yet, have no permanent address in New Zealand, then New Zealand Post can set up a Private Box or Private Bag at a post office in the city or town you plan to use as a base when you arrive in the country. Many organisations within New Zealand will accept either of these private addresses as an official address.

PENSIONS

Much has been published in the press regarding pension related problems. This remains a potential minefield to the average person, for which professional advice should be sought. You are required to declare all worldwide income including pension payments that will almost certainly be subject to further taxation in New Zealand under most circumstances, even if you are paying tax on it in the UK.

A Double Taxation Agreement is in place between the two countries, but as you are resident in New Zealand for tax purposes, they have the primary taxation rights over your income. Some countries have an agreement, particularly in relation to pensions, where only the country making the payment has sole taxation rights. Unfortunately, New Zealand is one of the few countries that does not have this agreement with the UK, so pension received must be declared as part of your worldwide income.

There is an option to take a 'pension payment holiday' in the UK that effectively ceases your contribution indefinitely and puts the pension on ice until the holding company receives further instructions. Transfer of existing pensions is always possible. We were asked about any holdings we may have had in the UK by our bank in New Zealand on the day we opened our accounts. This seemed a somewhat strange, but very direct, question to ask and was not particularly timely, but there appears to be more interest in pensions in New Zealand than in the UK. However, thorough research is still advised before committing to any form of transfer.

FAMILY CREDITS AND BENEFITS

This was the one area where red tape seemed to completely outweigh any modicum of common sense, not that this should come as any real surprise where UK government agencies are involved!

A simple enquiry by telephone some three months before emigrating, to determine how to stop payment of child benefit into our bank account, resulted in a declaration by the department stating that benefit payments would cease immediately. The telephone call was deemed to be enough to trigger a 'change of circumstance' and further investigations by the agency would need to be conducted. As an upstanding, law abiding citizen, I found this very intimidating, especially when informed that the agency investigations were to determine where I was going and why I was leaving the country!

My somewhat curt and frank response was to inform the agency that this was in fact none of their business and not to expect any answers to such personal questions. Following up the call with a letter to the head of the agency on the same day resulted in confirmation that the benefit would cease on the Monday after we had left the country.

The moral of the story is not to be too hasty in making enquiries of benefit agencies. Giving a week's notice should be plenty of time, given that they seem to be perfectly capable of stopping benefit on receipt of a phone call three months before you intend leaving the country. If they can do this then they can stop it within a week is the rather cynical view that I took!

INLAND REVENUE

Hindsight is a wonderful thing and I now realise that starting the liaison with the Inland Revenue early, to ensure everything is in order before leaving the country, is absolutely essential. Details of conversations or correspondence should all be logged to an individual file at the Inland Revenue, so any advisor who answers your calls should be able to scan a file history without the caller having to recite the whole story again and again. This is not always the case, however, and continually having to explain your individual circumstances is frustrating, annoying and does nothing more than add to the list of challenges to be resolved.

Dealing with UK tax issues from New Zealand is certainly not recommended, if only for the peace of mind from full settlement of your affairs prior to departing from the UK. The long telephone calls at ridiculous hours of the day – remember the 12-hour time difference – and waiting for responses to letters can be avoided with careful planning. Our situation was slightly different from many as our tax issues primarily revolved around a small business, but it still took almost 12 months after leaving the UK to sort out.

BANK ACCOUNTS

Managing a UK bank account from New Zealand is easy, especially with the abundance and ease of on-line accounting, but you may have no need to keep a UK account running. A debit card linked to the account can be used in New Zealand for ATM withdrawals, but transactions are treated as international transfers so purchases or withdrawals will attract commission charges for exchange of sterling to NZ dollars. Debit cards are not compatible with the EFTPOS system (see below) so be aware that you cannot swipe the card and use your UK PIN to confirm the transaction.

If you do elect to keep an active UK account, there is probably no need to continue receiving monthly statements. It may not be necessary to raise statements at all if on-line banking facilities are available – the choice is entirely your own.

Ensure there is a facility, preferably on-line, to transfer funds from the UK without having to raise further paperwork from New Zealand. Some banks require submission of a foreign currency transfer form on every occasion when funds would be moved to New Zealand. This means taking a supply of the forms with you and sending them back to the UK via airmail. The inevitable delays can be frustrating. On one occasion a form we despatched never arrived at our bank, resulting in the expense of follow up telephone calls and an even longer delay in transferring what turned out to be urgently required funds.

New Zealand banking is light years ahead of the UK. Ninety-five per cent of the population do not have any need to carry hard cash as they use an

EFTPOS card (electronic fund transfer at the point of sale) for purchasing just about anything. It is a simple system of swiping the card, punching in the PIN number at the till and, once accepted, the debit is immediately reflected on the bank account attached to that card.

The reason that the country is so technically advanced stems from a trial conducted some years ago to ascertain the effectiveness of the EFTPOS system. New Zealand was selected for the trial, not only because of its Western style technology but its comparatively small population. The system has become so well established that even taxis now utilise mobile communications technology for linking into the EFTPOS system to authorise payment by debit or credit card. The chequebook is now considered outdated and many outlets, ranging from supermarkets to petrol stations, no longer accept cheques unless by prior arrangement with the management.

The main banks all have comprehensive information on their respective websites. We elected to open an account with the ASB, which has been extremely helpful and efficient but personal preference was the only deciding factor. We were informed that funds are not normally transferred direct from the standard UK high-street account to a New Zealand account without first being lodged in a clearing account, normally based in London, as the accounting method in both countries is entirely different. There is a set fee for any transaction, whether the transfer amounts to £100 or £100,000, so at least the sliding scale of percentages does not apply in this case. Some of the major banks that operate in New Zealand are:

- ASB

- Westpac

- Bank of New Zealand (BNZ)

- The National Bank

- KiwiBank (operated through Post Shops).

5

Pets

If you intend to export pets to New Zealand you need to prepare for a hugely complicated, expensive and time consuming process that is almost guaranteed to try the patience of anyone! It really needs an expert and the best piece of advice is simply not to try to cut any corners.

There are some rather delicate issues that can arise from the export of pets, especially where children and older pets are involved. To be perfectly blunt but realistic, export of pets is really only applicable to cats, dogs and horses because veterinary clearances for Gordon the Goldfish or Harry the Hamster are highly unlikely to be made, even if they do exist! It is of the utmost importance therefore that the 'disposal' – in the nicest possible sense – of any family pets that children may be lovingly attached to is discussed very early in the plan. It should certainly feature on your spidergram as a key issue.

Consideration will have to be made for pets that are approaching the end of their expected lifespan and may not be able to cope with the travel, relocation or veterinary testing. Early consultation with a vet is highly recommended.

The export of our two West Highland white terriers was put down as just another necessary expense to achieve our goal, as my wife was adamant that she would not be going without them. I suppose I could always have left them behind and … not a chance!

EXPORT REGULATIONS

The following is a summary of the main points that need to be addressed, but in no way should this be considered as complete:

- Pet travel requires the use of an International Air Transport Association (IATA) approved air kennel that will provide enough space for the animal to stand up without touching the top of the box, lie down and turn around.

- Pets must be shipped as manifest cargo and not as excess baggage.

- An official Export Health Certificate (available from DEFRA) must be completed and stamped by your local vet.

- On two occasions, 14 days apart but within 30 days of export, faecal samples must be taken from animal(s) and examined for hookworm eggs. A government or veterinary institute laboratory must complete all tests for this condition and the results must accompany the Export Health Certificate.

- Treatment for internal parasites must be given within 21 days of export and again within 96 hours of export.

- Treatment with an insecticide dip for external parasites must be administered between ten days and two days of export.

- In the case of dogs only, blood tests/treatment for *brucella canis*, *dirofilaria*, *ehrlichia* and *leptospirosis* must be submitted to the relevant authority within 30 days of the flight with negative results. If any of these conditions prove positive then further tests/treatment must be conducted before the animal is allowed to travel. All blood tests must accompany the Export Health Certificate.

- A clearance of notifiable diseases certificate (Form EC618 or 618NDC) from DEFRA must be completed by a portal vet, i.e. at the transit kennels where the animals will travel from immediately before being loaded onto the flight. This form must accompany the Export Health

Certificate as your own vet only can complete the first two parts; the portal vet completes the remaining part.

New Zealand MAF requires pets to be tested for *babesia gibsoni* (a tick borne disease). A single drop of blood from the ear capillary must be taken and a thin, wide smear air dried on a slide and sent to the laboratory. This is to be conducted no earlier than ten days before the planned flight.

Phew! If you can get to grips with all this and more, and successfully complete the mountain of paperwork that goes with it then you are either a genius or a vet! As indicated at the head of the chapter, this is work for experts, so prepare to spend money if you intend exporting animals.

A simple table of veterinary requirements and paperwork is as follows:

	Import permit	Rabies	Other vaccines	Blood tests	Other tests	Microchip required
Cat	Yes	Optional	Optional	No	Yes	Yes
Dog	Yes	Optional	Optional	Yes	Yes	Yes

Fig. 7. Veterinary paperwork requirements.

BUDGET

The total cost of all testing, transit kennel fees, manufacture of flight kennels and the flight itself for our two Westies amounted to approximately £3,000. Note that this cost does not include boarding kennel fees of any duration, other than those for the transit phase to the airport, or cover the cost of treatment should any be required.

Despite some very detailed research beforehand, we were unable to source any rental homes in the immediate area of New Zealand where we intended to settle that would accept animals. So unless the intention is for pets to be lodged in boarding kennels on arrival in the country, the best solution is to leave them in the UK until you are ready to receive them. This of course does not apply if you are fortunate enough to be moving into your own house on the day that you arrive in the country, but that would be a highly unlikely situation given the requirement and timescale for your container full of goods to clear customs, coupled with the import processes requiring your signature against the release paperwork. Add to that the jet-lag factor, which normally takes at least three or four days' recovery time and the picture is clear. It is far from a sound idea to arrange for your pets to arrive on the same flight as yourself into your new country of residence: they will demand a great deal of attention and do not seem to suffer from jet lag. Believe me you will not regret this piece of advice!

In our case, bearing in mind the delay with selling the house, we spent nine weeks in rented/motel accommodation before moving into our own property. Even then there was a need to build some fencing around the house in New Zealand to make it secure for the dogs. This delay meant that they were lodged in kennels for the whole period before they finally left the UK, but the cost was minimal as the breeder from where they were bought volunteered to look after them and even transported them to the transit kennels when the time arose. The full cost for two dogs to stay in kennels over a two-month period will be expensive and is a further consideration in calculating the budget needs for your emigration programme.

TRANSIT KENNELS

The transit kennel will organise everything to do with paperwork, air kennels, transfer to the airport and flight details, and their involvement is a very necessary and important part of the equation. They will deal with the New Zealand authorities direct on your behalf and your only involvement will be to part with a cheque or credit card number for payment to get the process under way. This should also cover the cost for the transport of your pets to the transit kennel if that service is offered as well. A good dog breeder should be able to recommend an efficient transit kennel, but an internet search will provide a fairly comprehensive list.

FLIGHT INFORMATION

Once your pets are put onto a flight, they are not taken off the aircraft or released from their air kennel until arrival at their destination, the paperwork has been completed and you have signed to take delivery of them. Any animal in transit is visually checked at whatever stopover points may be scheduled, for their general health and that sufficient water is available, but they are not fed.

There are some myths and stories about air travel involving pets so here is some real information that we discovered in our research:

- Every pet travelling must have its own air kennel.

- Pets will not be allowed to travel on an aircraft when human remains are being carried.

- If horses or perishable foodstuffs are being carried, no pets will be carried in the same compartment.

- Pets are carried in a pressurised, heated, lit compartment similar to the passenger cabin (but with no trolley service!).

- Pets are not normally sedated on long haul flights. Most animals will sleep for a majority of the journey.

- Pets do not suffer from jet lag in the same way as humans do so be prepared for a lively companion on arrival in New Zealand.

It is possible that an animal booked on a specific flight may be moved at short notice to a later flight for a variety of reasons. The airlines are very aware just how sensitive the validity of certification is, and the potential cost involved if the export is delayed for any length of time.

Our dogs were flown two weeks before Christmas, when every airline but one was unable to carry them on the date required because of the large amount of Christmas hampers and fresh foodstuffs being ferried to New Zealand from the UK. The upshot of this was a last-minute increased cost by the airline involved because of demand, although we remain convinced that they were taking advantage of their lack of business in the hamper trade, perhaps attributable to their excessive freight charging policy! There is not a huge range of airlines to choose from anyway, so charges would be largely irrelevant, although seasonal effects can result in greatly increased fees.

ARRIVAL IN NEW ZEALAND

Auckland in the North Island and Christchurch in the South Island are the only commercial airports in New Zealand capable of taking Boeing 747 international flights, so passengers and freight are transferred to smaller aircraft for onward travel throughout the country.

Auckland tends to operate a majority of international 747 long-haul flights and so acts as the main gateway for pets arriving in the country. It is here that the initial import process is conducted to ensure that every last bit of paperwork is 100 per cent correct before your pets are released either for collection or further domestic travel. Once your pets arrive at their final destination, collection is invariably made from the cargo division at that airport and not from the conveyor belt in the terminal baggage hall, as some people would try to convince you!

New Zealand law states that all dogs must be registered annually with the local council for which the current fee is about $100 per dog if it has been neutered, or $140 if not. A numbered, coloured disc is issued that must be displayed on the dog's collar at all times. There are some stricter rules on ownership of dogs in the country than those that apply in the UK and a range of fines for infringements is rigidly enforced should you be caught out. One of the lighter offences is listed as 'failure to carry a dog leash in public', which will attract a fine of about £40.

That law appears to contradict the one that says all dogs must be kept on a leash in public, but the interpretation is largely centred on the control of dangerous dogs rather than two Westies enjoying their morning run down by the river.

As an aside, it is quite amazing to witness many dog owners arrive by car or truck at riverside walks, offload their dog(s) and then proceed to drive at speed so that their beloved pets will chase them. These bizarre activities do nothing for the reputation of a country of individuals who are renowned for maintaining an active and healthy lifestyle!

MICROCHIPPING

The law changed in 2006 and now states the need to microchip a dog if you are registering it for the first time in your local area. This is obviously applicable in your case as you are arriving as a new migrant. Once again there are some stiff penalties attached to non-compliance and failure to microchip a dog could result in prosecution and a $3,000 fine. There are some exemptions for working dogs, but domestic pets generally fall under this law. However, part of the export process now is the requirement to microchip your dog before it will be allowed entry to the country anyway, so the answer is to get it done sooner rather than later; another item for inclusion on your spidergram.

QUARANTINE

There are no quarantine requirements for animals arriving in New Zealand from the UK, other than keeping your pet(s) within the confines of a registered address for 28 days after the date of arrival. Taking dogs for a walk during this period, but restrained on a lead throughout, was deemed acceptable.

6

Getting There

There is much more involved in the travel part of your journey than just boarding a flight at London Heathrow and getting off in New Zealand. This chapter again reflects our own family experiences, but provides some food for thought and can be made part of your spidergram process so that nothing is left to chance.

FLIGHT PLANNING

There is a choice of airlines that operate the London to New Zealand route. Some have a single, short stopover in one country and others may make two or three. Specific carriers are British Airways, Air New Zealand, Qantas, Royal Singapore and Royal Brunei. You may also be able to find other routes direct to Australia with companies such as Virgin and then switch to a trans-Tasman flight from there, although travelling times will obviously be increased.

Many people we have met took the option of the London-Los Angeles-Auckland route because of the attraction of a stopover in LA to visit Disney World. If this is not your choice, and you want to travel direct to New Zealand in one go by the same route, then the flight to LA from London is about ten hours with a further twelve hours airborne to cross the Pacific into Auckland.

There is a higher luggage weight allowance on this route, of 32 kg per person for holidaymakers who are travelling down under. Our information was that for people flying on a one-way ticket as immigrants, the limit was doubled to 64 kg per person. Other routes have restrictions as low as 20 kg, so it is worth investigating before confirming bookings. The guideline is that each person checking in should have no more than two pieces of luggage to be placed in the hold, although we checked in a grand total of 13 items between the four of us with no penalty. Bearing in mind that we had no choice but to live out of a suitcase for three months, that much luggage was not regarded as excessive in our eyes. The airline you are flying with may see it differently, so confirmation of the latest rules and guidelines before you go would be a wise move.

UK TRAVEL

Take a moment to calculate the amount of space required in a vehicle for 13 suitcases, carry on baggage and four adults, and you will quickly realise that renting a one-way hire car from your home address to London is a complete non-starter. Family or friends may offer to drive you there but it could entail a small convoy of cars or even a mini-bus.

We opted for an airport 'coach-taxi' service that charges a flat rate from your home to the airport and for a journey of about 300 km the cost was £160 – a very reasonable £40 per person. Given that we were leaving the UK on a permanent basis, our choice was to spend a couple of 'tourist' days in London before flying to New Zealand, which proved to be a very refreshing and relaxing break.

Rail travel was considered, but the thought of arriving in London and having to travel to Heathrow with that much luggage was daunting. The sheer cost of one-way rail tickets compared with the taxi option effectively ruled out this mode of travel anyway.

PERSONAL CLOTHING

What clothing you take in your luggage is very much a personal choice, but bear in mind that the seasons in the Southern Hemisphere are completely opposite to those in the North. Leaving the UK in the depths of autumn and arriving on one of the warmest spring days recorded in

Wellington for many years was unexpected. However, arrival in Auckland at 5.30 in the morning, albeit only for a short time, was entirely different, as the sun had not yet come up and it was notably chilly.

The point of this is to highlight the dilemma in deciding the amount of warm clothing and outdoor coats to pack into the container, versus the amount that could be sensibly carried in our luggage on the flight. The key issue that will affect this phase of planning is the date on which your container will arrive in New Zealand and the allowance of ten to fifteen days for MAF clearance before the contents can be delivered to your house. It may be that you have to spend more than a few weeks in temporary accommodation so you will be living out of a suitcase. Regardless of when you travel, there is more than a reasonable chance that you will end up buying clothes when you arrive in New Zealand anyway, so why not consider travelling as light as possible and go shopping when you get there?

DOCUMENTS

Compiling an A4 travel file of original documents that have any connection with the immigration procedure or outstanding business in the UK, such as birth certificates, visa confirmation letters, bank correspondence, finance commitments, credit card details and so on, is an excellent way of putting everything you may need at your fingertips. Our file was kept out of the container as certain aspects of paperwork still had to be completed after the house had been packed and despatched to Southampton for shipping. Naturally, it accompanied us on our flight and the decision to take a briefcase as an item of carry on luggage containing just about everything connected with our immigration proved invaluable during our first two weeks in the country. There is something comforting about having all passports, driving licences, money and paperwork in easy reach, but this is obviously a personal choice.

MONEY

Until your New Zealand bank account has been formally activated and ATM cards have been issued, the only access to money will be what has physically been brought with you, supplemented by the use of a UK based bank account or credit card.

Activation of your New Zealand bank account is refreshingly simple. It takes about 30 minutes to complete the procedure at the customer services desk and you are issued with your ATM/EFTPOS card there and then. It is so much more efficient and friendly than the service offered by any UK bank, but you will obviously need to have transferred funds to New Zealand well in advance of your arrival so that they are at your disposal the moment your account is activated. Written confirmation of any funds transferred prior to you leaving the UK will be despatched by post to your UK address; it may well be useful to have a copy of these in your travel file in the unlikely event of any disputes.

The activation of our account eventually took place some five days after our arrival, because banks were not open at the weekend and the following Monday was a public holiday. Travelling with about $1,500 in cash is certainly not deemed excessive, but be aware that $5, $10 and $20 notes are used the most; $50 and $100 notes may not be accepted for smaller purchases.

Since we've been in New Zealand, our bank now opens seven days a week including a late night on Thursday, but not all mainstream banks have followed suit.

THE LA EXPERIENCE

In the wake of 9/11 and the increased security measures imposed at all US airports, the procedure at Los Angeles airport as a mere transit passenger was something I have never experienced in all my years of travel, but you just have to accept it.

We elected to make the journey to New Zealand in one go, but because our flight was booked through my military employers, we flew with Air New Zealand, routeing via the US.

The landing in Los Angeles involves a two to three hour stopover for crew change, refuelling, cleaning and resupply of the aircraft. Obviously, this could not be achieved without everyone leaving the aircraft so passengers are herded – and I choose the word carefully – into a very small transit lounge with basic toilet facilities, and complimentary coffee and cold drinks. After a ten-hour flight at least you could stretch your legs properly. However, the security guard who was marshalling passengers from the flight to the transit lounge was paranoid about people 'standing in a single line against the wall and not moving or you could be liable for arrest'. It was complete paranoia, but perhaps understandable given the terrorist attacks the country endured two years previously. I understand that passengers are also now required to undergo electronic fingerprint and eye scanning in addition to completing the required paperwork.

It took a little under two hours to complete the formality of 'entering' the USA and passports were duly stamped with an entry visa. All transit passengers were issued with a yellow disc, deemed so important by the security guards that announcements were made every few minutes to inform the 'captive' audience that loss of the disc would result in the offender being denied the opportunity to re-board the aircraft. The whole process is bewildering, given that every exit in and out of the transit lounge is locked and guarded. There is no opportunity for anyone other than the original occupants of the aircraft to get back on board anyway, so the issuing of a disc as some form of control remains a mystery.

Despite being assured that LA has some wonderful facilities – it was our intention to pay for a shower and have a meal in the terminal – there is no need to take US dollars for the journey as there is absolutely no chance of going anywhere in the airport to spend it. Smokers can forget any notion of a cigarette during the stopover, as smoking is prohibited everywhere inside the terminal including the transit area. At least the stopover was only a few hours.

HONG KONG

An excellent alternative to travelling via the US is to route through Hong Kong but still flying with Air New Zealand. The flight routine works the same as if you were going via Los Angeles in that you travel both legs of the journey in the same seat, but only if you are doing the whole trip without a break, of course.

The new international airport in Hong Kong is vast and boasts some amazing facilities including cafés, bars, shops and shower lounges, a good selection of which are within a few minutes of the Air New Zealand gate. During the three-hour stopover you are processed through immigration and are free to wander wherever you want in the airport until it is time to get back on the aircraft. This is so much more refreshing than the LA experience as it takes about 20 minutes from the moment you leave the aircraft to having the freedom of the airport; we are now firm converts to flying via Hong Kong on our trips to the UK. The opportunity of having a shower, freshly-cooked food and a cold beer before another 11 hours in the air is too good to pass up, but remember that the luggage limit is 20kg per person when routeing via Hong Kong. Smokers will be pleased to know that there are plenty of rooms located throughout the airport where you can indulge, but beware of getting too far away from your boarding gate as it takes about 40 minutes to walk from one end of the airport to the other.

These flights do get very busy and are normally full. Catering onboard has to account for both western and oriental passengers so don't be surprised to be offered pork in black bean sauce with crispy noodles for breakfast when the alternate choice of an omelette with sausage and tomato has run out.

7
Arrival in New Zealand

The flight finally arrives into Auckland and you set foot in your new home country where the air is guaranteed to smell fresher, cleaner and sweeter than it ever did in the UK. Despite your best intentions to go to bed on arrival, in a futile attempt to combat jet lag on day one, the excitement will be just too much and exploration will inevitably be the order of the day.

CUSTOMS/MAF

The bio-security policy in New Zealand has already been mentioned, but it is worth noting that there are some very strict rules in what can and cannot be brought into the country. Very polite and friendly MAF officials, together with detector dogs, greet the people and luggage arriving on every international flight to New Zealand. They are extremely professional and very efficient at their job, but any attempt to circumvent the system, or worse, smuggle a prohibited item into the country, is treated as a serious offence and you will face a very hefty fine if convicted. Failure to declare a single apple resulted in a well-known film star being fined $300, which happened not long after our own arrival in the country.

Some tips on how you should prepare for inspection should it be necessary are:

- Pack everything that you think may need to be inspected together.
- Use a separate bag, your hand luggage or pack it near the top of a suitcase.

- Try not to travel with food unless it will be consumed before arrival in New Zealand.

- Food for children and young babies should be kept handy and declared.

There are some particular issues with certain products that should be noted before travelling. In general, fresh, perishable foodstuffs such as fruit and meat are prohibited. In most cases official documentation will be required to allow entry.

Meat products

Products such as beef jerky, salamis and Chinese sausages are manufactured from dried meats, which have not been through any process to destroy diseased organisms. New Zealand's greatest threat comes from foot and mouth disease and the virus can survive for long periods in meat products. Should an outbreak of this virus occur in New Zealand, it would immediately halt the valuable export of meat and animal products and effectively destroy a huge part of the economy.

Honey products

Each year more than 20 million dollars worth of honey and bee products are exported from New Zealand, but the industry is worth much more to the country than just this. Fruit trees, flowers and vegetable crops rely on honeybees for pollination so the country's beekeeping industry must be protected. Honey is an unprocessed product and a potential carrier of bee diseases that could be unique to another country.

Dried edible plant products

An inspection of this type of product is required to ensure no insects are present. In some cases certain conditions of importation apply. All nuts for eating, particularly those in shells, require inspection.

Fresh fruit and vegetables

These are generally prohibited due to the risk from fruit fly. Strict import rules apply for bulk importers and MAF officials will find the apple or banana secreted in your hand luggage. If you should be provided with fresh fruit as part of the aircraft refreshment service, don't be tempted to keep it for a snack once on the ground in New Zealand.

Dairy and egg products

Restrictions apply to most dairy products, and fresh eggs and egg cartons are completely prohibited.

The best advice is to either travel with nothing or leave anything that may be of interest to MAF on the aircraft. Be totally honest if you are stopped on the way through the airport. We witnessed a lady who could not understand why she had been stopped, but the sniffer dog had detected food remnants on her baby's bib and it was duly confiscated for destruction (the bib – not the baby!).

HOTELS AND MOTELS

While there are major hotels in the big cities, regional hotels and motels located away from these areas tend to be a lot smaller and less formal. The few that were available in the area where we wanted to settle could not offer a suite of rooms suitable for family use, which is something we really needed as we were unable to buy our house in New Zealand because our own in the UK had yet to sell. The only alternative was to rent two separate units, an unexpected expense that did not feature in our budgeting plans, but probably could have been avoided with some extra research.

As a guide, a family of four staying in a motel for seven weeks costs around £3,000 for accommodation only. Unexpectedly, most of our accommodation expenses ended up being covered anyway, but the final bill was still a shock and would have dented our budget severely had we been required to pay the full amount.

If your intention is to use either a hotel or motel for any period on arrival into the country, it will be beneficial to do some internet research beforehand. In today's world of modern communications, most will have an email address for use in establishing room rates, discounted deals and facilities on offer.

Holiday homes are an alternative, but can be expensive to rent on a short-term basis. A typical three-bedroom home with all bedding and towels provided can cost anything upwards of £500 per week, depending on location, but this may be a viable alternative to motel costs if the size of your family demands it.

PUBLIC TRANSPORT

There are differing views on the efficiency of public transport across New Zealand, although the majority seem to think that services in general are reasonable. Bus services in the cities and major towns are certainly adequate, but traffic congestion can affect the timetable during peak hours – what city in the world is any different?

Rail services are quite efficient, but limited in terms of routes. Remember that New Zealand is a mountainous country and its railway lines are no more than single track in many areas and restricted in speed accordingly; don't expect anything like an Inter-City 125 service. Generally, routes tend to follow main roads where possible, as this is logically where most of the populous will settle. Most commuter line railway stations other than those at interchanges are rudimentary to say the least; nothing more than an up and down line platform with a large version of a bus shelter placed in the middle and no toilet facilities!

Taxis are numerous in the main cities, but not particularly cheap in terms of dollars versus income – a 20-minute ride home at the end of a night out can cost a day's wages for some people.

Queenstown, © Chee Kong See Thoe/iStock

Coromandel Peninsula, © Joe Gough/iStock

Lake Matheson, © Eldad Yitzhak/iStock

Track to Mount Cook, © Glenn Maas/iStock

Volcanic lake, © Ralf Herschbach/iStock

Mermaid pools, Tutukaka coast, © Scott Espie/iStock

Road to Milford, © Eldad Yitzhak/iStock

Lady Knox Geyser, Rotorua, © Adam Booth/iStock

Auckland, © Mike Morley/iStock

Rotorua, © James Scully/iStock

Lake Matheson © vyruz/iStock

Bay of Plenty, © Harris Shiffman/iStock

8
House Hunting and Buying

Looking for and purchasing the house that will eventually become your first home in New Zealand is much simpler than you are perhaps used to. There is normally a wide variety of properties available on the market, but the way in which houses are bought and sold differs a great deal from in the UK. The hints and tips in this chapter are important to ensure that your purchase does not turn out to be a disaster.

DECIDING WHERE TO LIVE

As with any country in the world, there are geographical areas in New Zealand where many people would choose not to live and, of course, there will always be the run-down areas that have a less than respectable reputation and higher incidents of crime than others. It is a sad reflection of modern city life that virtually anywhere you go on the planet has similar problems to those prevalent in certain areas of the UK except, in the case of New Zealand, on a much smaller scale.

The overriding factor for deciding where you might wish to live will be largely dictated by where you work. For example, we live in the Upper Hutt district, which is about 30 km north of Wellington and is well served by both road and rail routes. Rush hour traffic flows on State Highway 2, the main route in and out of Wellington, can vary considerably. However, housing in Upper Hutt is lower priced than that of the same standard in Wellington, so you will obviously get more property for your money. The drawback of this is that you have no option but to face the daily commute in and out of the city if that is where your workplace is, which can quickly become both tedious and costly. A monthly rail pass will cost around $160 and parking in Wellington costs anything from $10 – $15 per day depending on what time you arrive; anything after 8:30am is likely to be charged at the upper end of the scale, but only if you can find an empty space – premium parking is filled very quickly. This is almost certainly the case in other major cities so it would pay to research just what parking may be available in the area in which you would like to settle.

It is wise to look very closely at the local infrastructure, as well as doing some fairly in-depth research on the prospective area where you might be looking to settle, in terms of schooling and other key activities.

PUBLICATIONS

There are several free publications available weekly throughout the country dedicated to properties for sale in the housing market. The largest of these is probably The Property Press and is normally found in large dispenser baskets outside estate agents, supermarkets and shopping malls. Local 'free' newspapers are delivered direct to your letterbox and usually contain a reasonable selection of properties, although there is never room to publish every single one. Regional 'national' newspapers also carry a Residential and Business Property section once a week, but tend to run with the more expensive properties, given the associated cost of advertising.

We investigated whether or not publications such as this could be posted overseas, to the UK in particular, but the cost of this overrides their usefulness, as they are effectively out of date almost as soon as they are printed.

INTERNET

This is by far the most productive medium, where you will be able to find and view detailed pictures, both inside and out, of properties that may interest you. Just about every property that comes on the market can be found on a website somewhere and all are easily accessed simply by entering *real estate + New Zealand* into an internet search engine.

There are sites operated independently from an agent's individual site featuring a huge range of properties. The most well known is at open2view.co.nz and is packed full of useful tools and search facilities. Each property advertised on the site is accompanied by as many as 20 individual photographs and key details linked to the property. Some even provide 360° virtual views of the property section (garden), outdoor views and indoor rooms.

However, there are some things that should be remembered when viewing property details, the main ones being:

- Photographs are taken with a fish-eye lens so the size of rooms and objects will appear to look bigger than they actually are.

- If a section size is shown, but the floor area of the property is not, it may be an indication that the house is quite small. The buildings of a reasonably sized, four-bedroom home with single garage will cover an area of about 130 sq mtrs.

- The listing agent's description of some properties can be a long way removed from the truth, e.g. 'some work required' when they mean 'major work required'. Real estate jargon appears to be no different from that in the UK.

- The pricing of some properties is designed to get potential purchasers through the front door, but the vendor may well be looking for a price that could be as much as ten per cent higher than advertised.

- Some houses are advertised as being close to local amenities and schools, but fail to describe the ten-minute drive up extremely steep hills that are not on any public transport routes.

The largest high-street estate agents in New Zealand are:

Professionals	**www.professionals.co.nz**
Remax (Leaders)	**www.leaders.co.nz**
Harcourts	**www.harcourts.co.nz**
L J Hooker	**www.ljhooker.com**
First National	**www.firstnational.co.nz**
Bayleys	**www.bayleys.co.nz**

BUILDING INSPECTIONS AND REPORTS

'Buyer beware' is a term that means there is no redress except in the case of intentional fraud amounting to crime. This caveat is very much part of the sales and purchase business in the housing market and merits further explanation.

Buying a house is a huge investment that obviously needs to be safeguarded and one method is to have a property professionally inspected before purchasing. As house buyers in New Zealand operate in a 'buyer beware' environment, the long-term results could be disastrous if this course of action is not taken.

The potential pitfalls of buying a property without having it inspected first are many. One major source of excessive costs is as a result of the amateur DIY brigade who carry out alterations to houses in a generally unskilled fashion. Whilst the alterations may make the house look cosmetically stunning, there are many documented cases of dangerous side effects to structural safety.

A pre-purchase inspection is deemed essential as the identification of problems that will incur high maintenance costs enables the potential purchaser to make a considered judgement on the building. The advantage of this is that any immediate or ongoing costs can be set against the cost of a property during purchasing negotiations, or accepted by the vendor as their responsibility to remedy prior to sale. Yet despite the cost of this inspection being minimal in terms of the purchase cost, a surprisingly small number of people ask for this to be completed. To put this into context, there are probably more people in New Zealand who insist on a pre-purchase check-up of a car that in reality is worth no more than five per cent of the average property, yet for some reason have no desire to apply the same criteria for buying a house; more about cars later.

A further problem is that some vendors and real estate agents will on occasions deliberately discourage buyers from a pre-purchase inspection, for fear of losing a sale. The bottom line is that 99.9 per cent of individuals have absolutely no idea what to look for in assessing the market value and structural quality of a house. Therefore, if they are persuaded to forego a building inspection, they stand to potentially spend thousands in remedying faults. The cost of employing a professional to do that for you amounts to about £100 and can save huge amounts of money in years to come, especially if any major alterations have not been permitted by the council planning department.

For example, in our own quest to buy a house we viewed a property that had an extensive garage and sleep-out added on, but without planning permission or permission from the council. Effectively, such a building is not recognised as contributing to the value of the property so the insurance company would not acknowledge the structure as an integral part of the house. In the event of damage through fire, flood or earthquake, the insurance would not have paid out to rebuild that particular part of the property.

Land Information Memorandum

A LIM report is prepared by the local council and provides information on:

- Official address, legal description, area of site and unit/flat number as appropriate.

- Private and public storm water and sewerage drains.

- Government valuation and any rates that may be owing on the land.

- Consent, notice, order or requisition affecting any building on the site.

- Building certificates issued on the property.

- Use to which the land may be put.

- Special land features including potential erosion, subsidence, slippage and flooding.

From this list you will see that a LIM is very useful in helping to decide whether the land is worth purchasing and will be free from any restrictions. The report may well contain information about planned construction of a four-lane bypass at the end of the garden so is certainly worth the purchase price, again of about £100. Alternatively, you should be able to visit the local council offices and ask to see the building packet for any address within their jurisdiction as this will contain most, but not all, of the information featured in a LIM.

LEGAL PROCESS

The following is a brief outline of the legal process required for buying a property in New Zealand. As with other critical information that could affect both your wealth and health, further legal advice should be sought before committing to any form of purchase contract.

Preparation of an offer

There are key details that must be determined before an offer can be submitted, and the listing agent should take time and care to compile a contract in accordance with your wishes. Some of the more important factors are as follows:

- purchase price

- deposit (usually ten per cent)

- unconditional date

- settlement (possession) date

- chattels/furniture passing on the sale

- special conditions (subject to finance, LIM report, builder's report, valuation and sale of existing property if applicable).

Documentation

Once the terms and conditions of the contract have been agreed and meet your approval, they need to be incorporated into a formal offer document. The Real Estate Institute and District Law Society have prepared an Agreement for Sale and Purchase Form that is now in its seventh edition, and is widely accepted and appropriate for a majority of transactions. The wording of this agreement is critical and, while the real estate agents are very competent in completing the contract for presentation to the vendor, it is recommended that a solicitor checks the wording before signing as it may be too late afterwards.

The contract

Once the contract has been presented to the vendors it will either be accepted, rejected or negotiated through mutually agreed amendments. In our experience the latter is the normal course of action, because a potential purchaser will generally offer a figure equal to or marginally over that advertised by the vendor. One particular property we were interested in was advertised at buyer enquiries over £110,000. Our offer was made at £2,000 above that in an effort to conclude a quick sale, but the contract presented back to us by the agent had been amended by the vendor and the purchase price read £132,000.

This was a complete nonsense given that the government valuation of the property was listed as only £105,000. To put that into perspective, the difference in New Zealand dollars between the advertised and expected sale price amounted to nearly £23,000. Needless to say, we had no further interest in buying that particular house, but it is a salutary lesson that the vendors marketed the property in this way purely to gain people's interest. This is by no means an isolated incident.

Post-contract

Once the contract has been signed and dated, the agent sends signed copies to the solicitors of both the vendor and the purchaser. The purchaser's solicitor will immediately obtain a search of the title and any relevant documents recorded against the title. Copies will then be provided to the purchaser.

Conditions

At this stage the purchaser may be obliged to meet some of the conditions laid down in the contract. If the purchase is subject to the successful sale of an existing property then the contract will be dated to about six weeks ahead, by which time the purchaser must confirm the contract as unconditional or mutually negotiate another date. This action is carried out between the nominated lawyers for both vendor and purchaser. You should be absolutely certain that all conditions are met to your entire satisfaction before making the contract unconditional, because once you do, you are committed to completing the purchase. Any move to pull out of the contract after this stage can result in hefty penalties of up to 50 per cent of the purchase value stated in the contract, and will certainly affect your health and wealth!

Inspection

Prior to settlement/possession, the purchaser should ideally undertake to inspect the property to ensure that no damage has been done and that all chattels are in the same condition as at the date of first agreeing the contract. If the inspection reveals any anomalies then the purchaser's solicitor should be notified immediately through your own legal representation.

Settlement/possession

On the settlement/possession date, the purchaser's solicitor uplifts the loan advance (mortgage), and any cash contribution and pays over the full settlement figure by way of a bank cheque. The purchaser is entitled to vacant possession of the property as soon as moneys have been paid over, but not before, very similar to the final process that takes place in the UK.

Chattels

The items that are normally bought and sold with a house in New Zealand include stove, range hood, hob, dishwasher, curtains, blinds, drapes and light fittings. Fridge, freezer and microwave are not part of the chattels and if you are considering buying a house with a spa pool, for instance, expect separate negotiation to purchase these items from the vendor unless they are formally listed as included in the purchase price of the property. Check the contract very carefully – it pays to scrutinise the chattels section.

OPEN HOME

A unique way of presenting a house for sale in New Zealand is by conducting an open home. What this means is that the house for sale is open at a specific time on a specific day so that anyone can come in and view, but the vendors are not present because the estate agent who has marketed the property covers the event. This is normally done once per week at a prearranged time and the details are included in the weekly advertising placed by the vendor's estate agent. Most open homes are scheduled to take place at the weekend, but during the summer there are some that open mid-week in the evening, the whole thing lasting anywhere between 30 minutes to two hours, depending on location and the agent's recommendation. The agent will arrive at the house about ten minutes before start time and put up a company flag by his or her car to indicate that there is an open home taking place at that property.

Open home achieves by far the biggest percentage of sales in the market, but there are some negative points about the process that vendors don't like and some will insist on viewing by appointment only. Bear in mind that should a vendor opt for an open home once a week, their house will need to be cleaned for maximum impact during the presentation. Experience demonstrates that it takes a good two or three hours to achieve this on a Sunday morning for an open home that afternoon, so the vendor may not wish to do the same during the week.

Using the open home scheme

Planning your route around open homes that may be of interest to you is essential, to maximise the potentially short time available for viewing at each location. Be aware that it is common practice in New Zealand for visitors to remove their shoes before entering someone's house, whether it is an open home or not.

The agent conducting the open home will ask you to sign a register for insurance purposes, but this also doubles as a follow-up contact list for the agent to gauge your reaction to the property and whether you may have an interest in making an offer. If you do not wish to receive a follow up then make it clear to the agent when you leave that the property is not what you are looking for and ensure the register reflects those details. Honesty is by far the best policy and if a house does not meet your expectations then tell the agent why.

This scheme is a superb way of looking at lots of homes, but in popular areas some houses are on the market for a matter of days and never have the need to conduct an open home. Registering your interest with several companies may be an option, but be prepared for lots of recommendations – usually in the form of telephone calls – from the agents to view homes that have been on the market for months. Make sure you ask them to explain exactly why they believe such a property may suit you when they have been unable to sell it to anyone else.

A useful tip is to compare the Open2View serial number of the property, if it has one, with the latest houses appearing in the market. There is likely to be a wide gap between numbers allocated during the current week and those of two months previous, for example. If this is the case, ask the agent how many viewings have taken place since the house was marketed and probe for the possible reasons it may not have sold.

Real estate agents live off the commission they receive from the sale of a property or section. Some pay a standing fee of circa $500 per week for the use of a desk and office facilities in a high street branch. They will work hard to sell the properties in their portfolio, even more so if they have been on the market for some time.

RENTAL PROPERTY

There is a high level of home ownership in New Zealand, so the rental market is perhaps less well served than in most other developed countries.

First appearances of a property can be deceptive, so a visit before signing a rental agreement is essential. Most rental properties are unfurnished except for a stove, laundry facilities, carpets and curtains. The landlord is not even obliged to provide heating, so be aware that parts of the country can get quite cold and some properties lack any credible hours of sunshine because of their physical location, especially during the winter months.

Demand for rental property is high and the best places will go very quickly in popular areas. Wellington and Auckland are the highest priced areas where a three-bedroomed house will cost on average about £150 per week.

Many real estate agents also deal in rental property and the fee for completing a rental contract will normally amount to the cost of one week's rent. Advertisements can also be found in local newspapers through private sources where no fee would be payable.

9
Education

No matter where you settle, education is a complex subject that could fill a huge book on its own. However, there are some marked differences in the standard of education taught throughout New Zealand compared with those in the UK and once again personal experience is probably the most effective way of highlighting what may be expected.

The New Zealand curriculum is formulated on students gaining academic and practical skills in the following seven essential learning areas:

- language and languages

- mathematics

- science

- technology

- social sciences

- the arts

- health and physical well-being.

To supplement or balance these areas, there are a further eight practical or 'essential skills':

- communication skills

- numeric skills

- information skills

- problem-solving skills

- self-management and competitive skills

- social and co-operative skills

- physical skills

- work and study skills.

NCEA SYSTEM

NCEA stands for National Certificate in Educational Achievement, for which there are four levels as follows:

- Level 1 – Year 11 students

- Level 2 – Year 12 students

- Level 3 – Year 13 students

- Level 4 – scholarship level taken by top Year 13 students only.

To be awarded the Level 1 NCEA a student will have to accumulate a minimum of 80 Level 1 credits (or points); for Level 2 it is 80 Level 2 credits and so on. These credits are gained by passing Achievement Standards (or Unit Standards), which are similar to a unit of work.

Each year-long course of study is divided into, and assessed by, five to nine Achievement Standards. The table overleaf illustrates the Year 11 maths syllabus and associated credits that can be gained.

So a student who passes all the Achievement Standards in the Year 11 maths syllabus will gain a total of 24 credits. Given that a typical Year 11 student will study a minimum of six subjects, it is perfectly feasible to cover 40 or more Achievement Standards across those subjects and gain a maximum of 144 credits. Remember that a student only needs to gain 80 credits to be awarded a Level 1 certificate.

1.1	Algebraic Equations	3 credits
1.2	Graphs	3 credits
1.3	Measurement	4 credits
1.4	Geometric Techniques	2 credits
1.5	Statistics	3 credits
1.6	Probability	2 credits
1.7	Number Problems	3 credits
1.8	Right-angled Triangles	2 credits
1.9	Geometric Reasoning	2 credits

Fig. 8. Year 11 maths syllabus credits.

Most of the assessments are done internally, i.e. by the teaching staff at the school or college, but this process is subject to sampling and moderation by the education authorities. External assessments include end of year examinations where up to four or five Achievement Standards in a particular subject are assessed.

The result for each Achievement Standard is reflected as one of four possible grades:

- Not Achieved

- Achieved

- Merit

- Excellence.

If the student is graded as Not Achieved in any Achievement Standard then no credits are awarded. Any other grade from the remaining three will earn the full amount of credits available for that Standard. In other words there is no middle ground; you either get full credits or none at all for any one Achievement Standard.

It is possible to carry across up to 20 credits from one level to the next, so if you earn 100 credits at Level 1 there is only a requirement to earn 60 further credits at Level 2 and still achieve a pass.

Certificates of Achievement are simple and reflect that a student has been awarded Level 1 NCEA, for example. There is no indication of how good (or borderline) the pass was, so potential employers are none the wiser about just what was achieved in school without asking for formal results sheets, although there is no obligation to do this. Until recently, certificates did not contain details of elements that were Not Achieved, but this has been changed to give employers greater visibility of exactly who has achieved what.

STATE SCHOOLS

There is a reasonable selection of state schools throughout New Zealand, although in my personal opinion, but backed by others I have met, there is evidence that the standard of education is lower than that achieved in the UK. The problem appears to revolve around a lack of quality teachers and the reliance on overseas staff to fill the gaps. On top of that, the quality of some of the gap-fillers leaves much to be desired, but there seems to be little choice other than to make the best of what is on offer.

A strong focus on sports activities fosters a competitive spirit between the various institutions and generates a real sense of pride in representing the school at any level. Students are actively encouraged to take part regardless of competency, which certainly boosts personal confidence and morale.

Attendance at some schools is governed by zoning rules and this has a marked effect on house prices within the zone, depending on the quality of the school. As is the case in the UK, some schools are better than others. Some residential properties are shamelessly marketed as being in a particular zone for a school that is in high demand and will be priced way over the value of a similar house half a mile down the road. If the job offer you receive is limited to a particular region then the choice of school may well be equally limited, unless boarding school is an option.

Most state schools and colleges charge nominal fees to fund what would be described as routine schoolwork in the UK. On top of this a voluntary donation of about £60 per year is requested for each student, but given that this is not mandatory, it appears that those who do contribute are in the minority. The general impression regarding voluntary donations is that taxation in the country is high enough already, and the government has plenty of surplus funds in reserve, so why should parents and, in particular, low-income workers have to pay for mandatory schooling?

Government educational reports on how well a school is performing can provide you with a valuable insight, but it must be taken into account that the measurement is done using a New Zealand benchmark, so it still might not reach the same standard as a UK equivalent institution. Promotional websites designed and maintained by the schools themselves are well presented and most will declare just how good their particular school is. However, it would pay to treat these with a degree of scepticism as the site is merely an advert intended to entice the reader. Visiting and touring the school will provide a much better physical insight than simply making a decision based on a web page. For example, the school our daughter attended praised itself on their wonderful standard of drama and the facilities available to achieve it. The reality was far from the truth, however, and the quality of both teaching and output was in fact way below the basic standard that had already been experienced in the UK.

Rules and uniform

The wearing of uniform is strictly enforced. Most major department stores stock a limited supply of school uniform, but many schools run their own shop and stock both new and used items. Schools are very much reliant on the money they raise from these outlets as this tends to provide a good source of income that balances the lack of 'voluntary' contributions in a lot of establishments.

In some schools and colleges where blazers are mandatory, parents have no choice but to buy them from the school shop and they have simply to accept that they will be sold at a premium price, as are all the other goods. We found that, in general, school uniform in New Zealand was more expensive than similar items in the UK, but this may differ between geographical areas of the country.

Cultural issues

Schools and colleges are obliged to accommodate various religions and cultures, particularly Maori, but there are ongoing political issues in New Zealand regarding rights of Maoris that continue to be reflected through the generations from grandparents right down to young children. The school authorities must perform a fine balancing act in recognising cultural practices. Whilst the promotion of harmony – certainly between Maori and other children – in educational establishments is a high priority, there is anecdotal evidence in some regions that this has been difficult to achieve.

A small yet significant example of this is related to the wearing of religious or family symbols – something that I can confidently comment on through family experience. Maori icons include pendants carved from either green or white stone worn around the neck, usually on a leather thong. These appear to be considered acceptable as the authorities do not want to be seen as imposing on age-old tradition, and quite rightly so. However, the wearing of a small cross on a chain by other pupils, a symbol commonly recognised on a worldwide basis, is deemed to be unacceptable in some cases as it represents nothing more than decorative jewellery. This interpretation inevitably results in accusations of favouritism, resulting in the scales becoming unbalanced and generating resentment.

The traditional Maori performing arts organisation known as Kapa Haka is recognised in all schools and across many other learning institutes throughout New Zealand. Unlike other indigenous dance forms, it is unique in that performers must sing, dance, have expression as well as movement all combined into each act. Kapa Haka could be interpreted as a form of sign language, as each action has a meaning designed to tie in with the words.

PRIVATE SCHOOLS

As with a majority of countries in the world, you have the option to pay for private schooling. There is a good choice of private schools although many are based around the major cities. The cost of such education is expensive in relation to the average wage structures. The typical cost for two children to attend private school on a non-board basis from 11 years and upward ranges from approximately £5,500 to £8,000 per year. This equates to $15,000 to $22,000 and is beyond the majority of parents who may only be earning an average wage.

TERTIARY EDUCATION

Further education after compulsory, secondary education is rarely free and can actually be more expensive than private schooling in some cases. This is especially true if you are intending to arrive in New Zealand on the Work to Residence Visa, as you are effectively a working visitor to the country, having not yet gained residency. There is no guarantee that you will gain residency or even elect to stay in the country, so the education establishments are bound to apply charges accordingly.

As such, anyone intending to study at tertiary level is normally classed as an international student and, depending on where the study is undertaken, the cost will almost certainly start around the $12,000 mark for a 32-week package at a polytechnic college. Expect the fee to rise further for university education. If you have two children who are at that level of study the fees could realistically top as much as $40,000 – a massive sum in relation to income.

There are some other drawbacks with the Work to Residence Visa in connection with education, in that tertiary students are not entitled to draw student loans or receive student allowances because they are not residents in the country other than for tax purposes. The government student allowance of about $150 per week would be very useful in helping out with incidental expense, but is not available to anyone who has not been a permanent resident in New Zealand for at least two years, despite the requirement to pay full taxes in the same way as everyone else.

There is clear evidence that a steadily increasing number of students in New Zealand rely solely on government loans to fund tertiary education courses. As recently as 2006 the total owing to the crown was approximately $7 billion, but this has risen to $10 billion in 2008 and continues to grow at an alarming rate of around $1 billion per year. This remains an attractive way of borrowing money because the government declared in 2006 that all borrowers in New Zealand would be exempt from interest on their loans; an obvious reason as to why the debt is increasing so rapidly. This figure reflects that more than 13 per cent of all young New Zealanders aged 15 or over are in debt. Of these, medical graduates and scientists owed the most and were top of the list to leave the country after gaining their qualifications in the search for a more attractive package in terms of pay. Nearly one in five graduates who owed more than £10,000 upon leaving study in 1997 were still overseas and almost half of Bachelor graduates have made no progress in repaying their loans.

Student loans are repaid through borrowers' taxes once that individual has started work. The current threshold for these repayments to commence is earnings more than $19,084 a year and salary earned above this threshold will result in higher repayments accordingly. It is an excellent scheme, but borrowers need to take into account their repayment levels once they start work and be prepared for a lean couple of years once they have completed tertiary education. This is especially true as I have met some people whose student loans totalled $70,000, which in this case was used to train as a helicopter pilot.

None of the comments in this chapter are intended to be controversial and were written to illustrate the marked difference in education standards, practices and cultural priorities in comparison with the UK. Much work is needed on your own behalf to research exactly what a school or college can offer. You should be ready to accept some fundamental changes in the educational outlook and expected results for your children.

Employment

Job opportunities in New Zealand are essentially no different from anywhere else. In the case of immigrants, the Government actively encourages skilled workers from overseas to fill particular positions, but with some clear rules and guidelines. Chapter 3 briefly touched on some of the basic factors to help in your decision making and this chapter provides more detail associated with employment processes and what you can expect from the New Zealand job market.

WHAT SKILLS?

There is a list maintained by the Department of Labour – the *Essential Skills in Demand List* – that provides general information about employers from across the whole of New Zealand who are looking to fill positions requiring particular skills. This list is reviewed every six months to ensure it accurately reflects current employment demands by adding or removing occupations and changing any qualification or experience requirements as necessary. This process is carefully conducted based on submissions made to the Department of Labour from key players in the employment market and other interested parties such as government departments, unions and nationwide training organisations. The *Essential Skills in Demand List* is divided into two distinctive sub-lists called:

- the Long Term Skill Shortage List

- the Immediate Skill Shortage List.

The Long Term Skill Shortage List (LTSSL)

This list reflects occupations that are recognised as being affected by a distinct shortage of skilled workers to fill a position both in New Zealand and world wide. The openings on this list are regarded as key positions to be filled, and prospective migrants who manage to gain employment in one of these areas will be considered for a work visa under the Work to Residence scheme. There are other benefits for those candidates who have work experience and qualifications that can be applied to the skill shortages on the LTSSL in that they may gain extra points towards their eventual application for permanent residence.

Occupational Groups	Occupation	LTSSL Requirements *Qualifications must be comparable to the standard of the NZ qualification listed.*	Specifications *(In order to claim bonus with regard to visa applications)*
Professional Occupations	Secondary school teachers	Bachelor's degree (or equivalent) with a major in a NZ teaching subject AND a secondary teaching qualification recognised for registration purposes by the NZ Teachers' Council OR a four-year Bachelor of Education or Teaching (Secondary) with a major in a NZ teaching subject	Bachelor's degree (or equivalent) with a major in a NZ teaching subject AND a secondary teaching qualification recognised for registration purposes by the NZ Teachers' Council OR a four-year Bachelor of Education or Teaching (Secondary) with a major in a NZ teaching subject
	Quantity surveyor	Bachelor of Construction (Quantity Surveying) AND three years relevant post-qualification experience	Bachelor of Construction (Quantity Surveying)
Health Groups	Registered Nurse	Bachelor of Nursing OR Diploma in Comprehensive Nursing, diploma or hospital-based certificate AND New Zealand registration	Bachelor of Nursing OR Diploma in Comprehensive Nursing, diploma or hospital-based certificate

Fig. 9. LTSSL example.

The following are key factors that have to be met before an occupation can be included on the LTSSL:

- there is an ongoing and sustained shortage of suitable workers in New Zealand and across the world

- the shortage is prevalent across the whole of New Zealand

- the occupation must meet the Skilled Migrant Category definition

- the salary for this post must be at least $45k based on a 40-hour working week.

The Immediate Skill Shortage List (ISSL)

Occupational Groups	Occupation	Recommended standard for work permit applicants with an offer of employment	Regions
Professional Occupations	Auditors	Degree level (Level 7) qualification majoring in accounting	Auckland, Waikato, Bay of Plenty, Central North Island, Wellington, Canterbury, Otago, Southland
	IT specialist	Bachelor of Science, with majors in computer science or information science AND a minimum of three years full-time with at least 12 months relevant work experience in the past 18 months	Auckland, Upper and Central North Island, Wellington, Upper South Island, Christchurch
Health	Dental Technician	Diploma in Dental Technology AND New Zealand registration	Auckland, Upper, Central and Lower North Island, Wellington, Upper South Island, Christchurch, Otago, Southland

Fig. 10. ISSL example.

This list differs from the LTSSL as it contains details of occupations where there is an immediate shortage of workers available in New Zealand. If a migrant can produce an offer of work in an occupation registered on the ISSL then the New Zealand Immigration Service will simply accept that there are no suitably qualified citizens or residents available to fill that post, which means a temporary work visa and permit can be granted without further question. The key points applicable to this list are:

- the occupation is deemed to be in a shortage category in New Zealand

- the geographic region(s) of the country where the shortage exists is clearly defined.

JOB VACANCIES

The inclusion of any jobs on either list is only considered after taking into account a range of factors that need to be confirmed before the post can be added. Some of the key factors are:

- the particular industry is committed to training New Zealanders

- domestic labour market resources must be exhausted before recruitment of overseas workers can be considered

- there is clear evidence of a prospective employer having difficulty recruiting and employing staff

- evidence of an estimated imbalance between new apprentices and trainees entering the profession against those leaving or retiring from the industry.

Prospective migrants must carefully account for the time it takes from applying for a visa against the possibility that a job may be filled from other resources while you are waiting for confirmation that your visa has been granted. The lists are reviewed every six months and the removal of a vacancy could have serious consequences on the issue of a visa.

OCCUPATIONAL REGISTRATION

In the sample lists above there is mention that in addition to educational qualifications there is a requirement for registration in some jobs. This means that people who intend to work in particular occupations in New Zealand are required by law to register with the associated professional body. This is intrinsically linked with your visa application as you will qualify for points under the Skilled Migrant Category if you have been granted full or provisional registration, which entitles you to legally work in that profession. In the case of dental or medical professionals you must hold written confirmation from the New Zealand Dental or Medical Council that you are eligible for full or provisional registration. Within one month of arrival in New Zealand you must undertake to attend a personal interview with a representative from the council body of your profession, in order for the registration to become valid.

The list of those professions requiring registration is comprehensive and has not altered much in the past few years, so the following is considered to be an accurate reflection for the purposes of this book:

architect	medical laboratory technician
barrister or solicitor	medical practitioner
chiropractor	medical radiation technologist
clinical dental technician	nurse and midwife
clinical dental therapist	occupational therapist
dental hygienist	optometrist
dental technician	osteopath
dental therapist	pharmacist
dentist	physiotherapist
dietician	plumber, gasfitter and drain layer
dispensing optician	podiatrist
electrician	psychologist
electrical service technician	real estate agent
enrolled nurse	land title surveyor
immigration advisor	teacher
medical laboratory scientist	veterinarian

JOB HUNTING

It may be stating the obvious, but the employment market in New Zealand is nowhere near as demanding as the requirements in the UK, but that is offset by a total population of only 4.2 million people. However, because of the global recession the country has experienced the same turmoil in its own job opportunities as most other developed countries and the available vacancies have dropped considerably. The numbers of employees being culled by businesses across the country in less-skilled jobs have increased as every effort is made to streamline operations to ensure future prospects. There are no clear figures of just how many people in this situation have managed to find other work but the numbers being made redundant on a weekly basis in 2009 was at the highest level for many years.

The changing picture

In the first edition of this book I mentioned that there were over 600 New Zealanders leaving the country every week in search of better paid work overseas. That trend appears to have now completely reversed and there is clear evidence that in mid-2009 people have been returning to the country in their thousands as they have been unable to secure or maintain employment overseas. There is anecdotal evidence of both New Zealanders and Australians finding it increasingly difficult to land any sort of casual work in the UK as jobs become harder to find. In most cases this involves the younger generation who are doing their Overseas Experience or 'Big OE' as it is known down under. Typically, these are people in their gap years from university and doing an OE is nothing short of a duty-bound pilgrimage to be achieved before settling down into a career.

Many of these people are likely to have some form of student loan, which is a government-sponsored scheme to cover tertiary education fees and is paid back through their income tax, according to how much they earn, once they start full time employment. Accordingly, most will be in debt when they really want to set out on their OE, so funding for a year's worth of travel is not easy to come by. A 'working holiday' is the obvious solution and London has, for a long time, been the most popular destination. It is a starting point where money can be earned doing short-term contracts or casual employment that in turn will fund the next part of their journey – Europe and onwards. However, according to employers in London, Australians and New Zealanders tend to make a commitment to work for a minimum of six months, for example, but often only stay for two months because they have earned enough to move on. This is not an ideal situation for employers who are in consequence taking on more young European workers trying to secure a long-term future in the country; this is clearly at the expense of those temporary workers from down under. The outcome is fewer jobs available and a greater flow of people back to Australia and New Zealand as they find it increasingly difficult to survive on what little funds they have; they also, of course, have no entitlement to social security benefits.

If any more statistics were needed to back up the huge increase in job applications in New Zealand against the number of jobs actually available, then take the case of the New Zealand Army. In May 2009 there were more than 7,000 applications to join the Army of which just over 800 were accepted. Over 6,000 applicants have been placed on a waiting list and the ceiling total from top to bottom of enlisted personnel required is only 5400. The moral of this particular story is that planning to join the Army as a new recruit is not a guaranteed option like it perhaps used to be, but there are certainly vacancies for individuals with specific skills and at particular ranks. Lateral recruiting from overseas is still active but in a much reduced capacity than it was only two years ago; this is also true of the other two services. The people on this list hoping for a call-up to join could potentially be waiting for two to three years and will have to look for other employment when they realise their prospects are not very good.

Whilst there would not be many migrants planning to come out to New Zealand just to join the Army, the knock-on effect is clear – more people hunting for fewer jobs in a market place that is not predicted to grow by any significant amount until at least the end of 2010. Graduate recruitment programmes have been subjected to some quite dramatic cuts with careers advisors at Massey, Victoria, Waikato and Otago universities saying that students in all subject areas are finding it tough to get work. One particular firm offered just 140 graduate positions in 2009 and received 3,000 applications for the posts.

JOB HUNTING TIPS

There are many tried and tested methods that claim to be better than the rest when it comes to landing the perfect job but there are four key steps that will boost your prospects wherever you may be in the world:

- thorough research into the potential opportunities open to you

- maintaining a well crafted and adaptable CV

- applying only for suitable jobs; and

- preparing and practising for job interviews.

In each of these steps there are some fundamental things to think about that are equally applicable in New Zealand.

Research opportunities

Since we immigrated to New Zealand there have been numerous occasions when we have discussed with other people how their job in the UK is nowhere near comparable to that in New Zealand when taking skills and qualifications into account. It is certainly helpful to try and talk to someone in the same field of work as they may be able to tell you exactly what types of job are suitable. This will in turn lead to current labour markets and where those types of job may be available geographically. Perhaps one of the most decisive factors that will influence what job you may be looking for is where you would like to live. You may prefer to settle in a bustling city, small town or out in the country, which will almost certainly determine what type of work will be available. Coupled with that is what you and your family's lifestyle activities are – skiing, hill walking (known in New Zealand as tramping), fishing, sailing, etc. It may well be that you would have to adjust your ideal lifestyle to one that ensures financial security by settling where there is more chance of getting the job you want.

Maintaining your CV

I have no intention of trying to preach about the 'perfect' CV as I am not sure that such a thing exists! Your CV is unique to you and your situation, therefore you owe it to yourself to spend some considerable time in creating a top quality document that will get you noticed. It is a well known fact that if a prospective employer cannot get a mental picture of your capabilities within the first two pages of a CV then it is likely to be put on the rejection pile. Many 'experts' say that a CV should be no more than two pages long anyway, as anything beyond that is largely regarded as just padding.

You should consider using written references and include appropriate contact details – ensure you ask your referees if they are happy for you to do that – especially as a prospective employer will have no way of confirming the accuracy of your CV given that you have not long arrived from the other side of the world. Some possibilities for a referee are your most recent employer, a member of a government or legal type organisation (military, Justice of the Peace, local MP, etc.), anyone who you may work with in a voluntary capacity (Red Cross, Salvation Army, Scouts, etc.) and lastly, a personal friend who is already living and working in New Zealand if, of course, you know someone who fits this category.

Application for jobs

It is a well known fact that many jobs are not actually advertised and people find out about them by word of mouth. This is very true in New Zealand and I have had personal experience of this very situation having been introduced to a new immigrant into the country at a social event. I spent some time talking about his reasons for moving to New Zealand and was surprised to discover that he didn't actually have a job to go to but was absolutely determined that he was not going back to the UK. His particular skill was something that just happened to be of interest to the military at that time and the end result was him landing a civilian contractor job for the military simply because I was able to put him in touch with the right people. A hint of pure fortune in this particular case, but this guy had to go through all the processes of gaining a work permit and ultimately residency whilst in the country, which I can assure you is not good for the stress levels.

You can do a great deal of homework before leaving the UK and enhance your prospects by signing up to job websites and registering with a recruitment company to help your case. There is usually no charge for this as most recruitment agencies work on behalf of the employers, and it is they who pay the required fees for the service. Average salary ranges are detailed earlier in the book.

CONCLUSION

The turmoil that has been a constant feature of global employment issues has certainly not yet been resolved and some experts have predicted that it will continue for 2–3 years before any real change in employment patterns and strategies are evident. The impact of world issues is being felt just as keenly in New Zealand as elsewhere and your ambition to emigrate will almost certainly have been dented at some stage by connected issues. By this I mean such matters as the cost of living increases, plummeting house prices, low exchange rates and the effect these things have on your plans. However, it is not insurmountable and your will to work around these issues will be testament to your determination to emigrate, no matter what!

11
Health Issues

No matter where anyone travels or lives in the world, there will always be concern over the provision of health care, both physically and financially. New Zealand has a health and disability system that is mainly funded by the government, so people who are ordinarily resident in the country are normally entitled to free or subsidised public health services. Publicly funded services include free care and treatment in public hospitals and highly subsidised treatment in the public or private health sector for accident victims. Nobody will be refused emergency care even if they are not a New Zealand resident.

DOCTORS

There are doctors and GPs practising in just about every town on the map, so the choice is very much down to the individual. Having said that there is an overall shortage in the medical profession because the loss of qualified doctors overseas to organisations offering far greater wages and benefits continues to be an ongoing problem. The main difference compared with the UK is that doctors conduct their surgeries as a private business, so you will pay for an appointment and the resultant prescription in a majority of cases.

There is a discount system in operation, which is officially known as the Community Services Card (CSC), but is also referred to as the 'Health Card', 'Exemption Card' or 'Discount Card'. The purpose of the CSC is to assist families on low or modest incomes to pay for their GP visits and prescriptions. Adults will receive up to £5.60 subsidy and children aged 6–18 up to £7.50. The card covers all family members, but there are thresholds set by the Ministry of Social Development on exactly who will receive what, as reflected in the following table:

Family size	Income threshold (before tax)
Single – living with others	$22,120 or less
Single – living alone	$24,514 or less
Married, civil union or de facto couple with no children	$36,618 or less
Family of 2	$44,211 or less
Family of 3	$53,539 or less
Family of 4	$60,959 or less
Family of 5	$68,225 or less
Family of 6	$76,346 or less
For families of more than 6	Increases by $7,154 for each extra person

Fig. 11. Discount thresholds.

If you do not qualify for any sort of discount, expect to pay an average fee of $45 per adult and $25 per child for a visit to your doctor. Prescriptions are subsidised by the government, although a part charge of up to $15 can be made per item, but there is usually no charge for children aged 6 years or under.

A referral from the GP is required to attend a hospital for a specialist appointment, but costs for private specialists and consultants will fall on the patient and not the government. There are some 445 hospitals in New Zealand at the last count, of which only 85 are publicly funded and run by District Health Boards. In view of this, many New Zealanders opt for health insurance as a necessity. If the insurance is affordable then access to private health care is available at the end of the telephone. However, you are still entitled to public health services even if you have private health insurance.

Insurance packages are available to cover most eventualities, including a routine visit to the GP in certain cases, and some employers offer such benefits as part of employment terms and conditions. Check what may be available to you and your family before committing to any private schemes.

Visits to physiotherapists, chiropractors and osteopaths attract government subsidies if your family doctor has referred you, but there are no subsidies on opticians' fees, or fees charged by natural therapists unless the therapist is also a doctor or midwife.

DENTISTS

Most adults have to pay for their dental care, and costs can run to hundreds of dollars depending on the work required. Basic dental care is available at no charge for children up to the age of 18 as part of a government subsidy scheme. However, dental surgeons have to register their participation in the scheme and many prefer not to take part. There is a good choice of dental surgeons throughout the country listed in the *Yellow Pages.*

It is said that the average New Zealander will visit the dentist only if it is absolutely necessary, because most do not get any sort of subsidy and treatment is once again expensive in relation to average wage levels.

Item	Cost
Examination and diagnosis	$60
Examination, x-ray and diagnosis	$90
Scale and polish (per 15 minutes)	$60
Single extraction under local anaesthetic	$120
Each additional extraction	$70
Single root filling (no restoration)	$330
Single filling (one surface)	$80
All ceramic crown	$1000
Full upper and lower dentures	$2500

Fig. 12. Typical dental work fees.

CHEMISTS

Generally referred to as pharmacies in New Zealand, chemists can be found in suburban areas, shopping malls or near medical establishments. If there is a need for medicine outside normal trading hours, this can be obtained from an Urgent Pharmacy. They are listed in the Hospitals section of the telephone book and are usually open until 10 or 11pm.

Pharmacists are able to offer a wide range of advice on the safety and use of medicines and there is more emphasis on the merit of this service than in the UK.

Television appears to play a big part in promoting the knowledge and skills of a pharmacist, as 'health updates' are run during advertisements, especially at peak viewing times. This is definitely something that is underestimated in the UK, and is an informative and interesting service delivered in the best interests of the population. It has been proven that this particular drive helps to maintain shorter waiting lists to see a doctor, as more people seek advice from their pharmacy. The fact that this service is free probably contributes a great deal to its overall success.

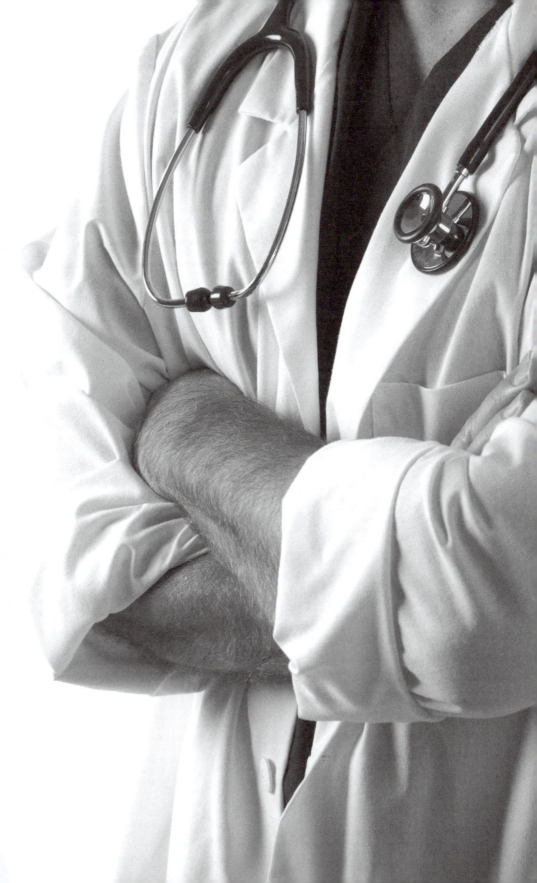

12
Cars and Driving

There is a great deal of information contained in country guide books about Kiwi driving standards, but it is hard to make any sort of preparations for the general style of driving simply from experience in the UK. One thing is without question, however: some drivers in New Zealand could be the nicest people you would ever wish to meet in the street but turn into aggressive and discourteous individuals when they get behind the wheel of a car. This is by no means an exaggeration and many New Zealanders I have spoken to openly agree with that view.

There seems to be an obsession with cars unlike anything experienced in the UK. The younger community in particular is let loose on the roads without any real driving experience and even less road sense. The inevitable outcome of this is increased traffic offences and, ultimately, often fatal accidents.

DRIVING LICENCE

The licensing system in New Zealand is very different from that of the UK as it still allows children to drive at the wise old age of 15. This condition was introduced when the school leaving age was raised from 14 to 15 in 1944 and has never been changed, despite the leaving age being raised to 16 in January 1993.

The initial licence is a learner's. It works in the same way as in the UK where the driver cannot drive the car on public roads unless someone who is in possession of a full licence accompanies them. A set of 'L' plates must also be displayed whilst the learner is driving and this licence can be issued to anyone 15 years or older. However, the applicant must first pass a road code examination, which is similar to the Highway Code written test in the UK.

The examination consists of a series of questions with multi-choice answers that are more a case of common sense than anything that may confuse. The road code is both book and CD based, although the CD is an interactive programme that also contains 12 dummy examinations in the same format that you will face when taking the test in New Zealand. The real test is made up of questions taken from across the range contained on the CD so, if you learn all the tests on the disc you will easily complete the test at the examination centre.

Once a learner has learnt to drive, an application is made to complete a road test. It takes no more than twenty minutes and merely assesses your general ability to drive safely. There is no set format for the test and whether you get to parallel-park, do a three point turn or reverse around a corner will depend on the mood of the examiner on the day. Providing the test is successfully completed the learner will become what is classed as a 'restricted' driver, for which some of the specific restrictions are as follows.

- Passengers may not be carried unless there is a supervisor sitting beside the driver who has held a full licence for a minimum of two years.

- Restricted licence holders are not allowed to drive between the hours of 10pm and 5am unless accompanied by a supervisor.

- A full driving test can only be applied for when a restricted licence has been held for a minimum of 18 months by anyone under the age of 25 years. If you are over 25 then you must hold a restricted licence for a minimum of six months.

Differences from the UK

Holders of a full UK licence may drive on their licence for one year only after the date of arrival in the country. Within this time, the holder must take and pass the road code test before application for a New Zealand licence can be made. The law states that your driving licence is to be carried at all times whilst you are driving. Failure to produce a licence as required by a police officer can result in an on-the-spot fine.

There are even differences in the scale of blood alcohol levels, depending on age. If you are under 20 years old then the limit is 30 mg per 100 ml of blood, effectively a zero limit. Consuming one drink will normally result in a driver being charged with drink driving. If you are over 20 years old, however, the limit increases to 80 mg per 100 ml of blood, but the guideline from the Land Transport Safety Authority (LTSA) says that your driving may well be affected before you reach the legal alcohol limit. The overall message is the same in New Zealand as in the UK – if you are going to drink, then don't drive.

A prominent national newspaper prints the names of drivers convicted for drink-driving offences together with the amount they were over the limit, the disqualification period, fine imposed and even the prison sentence or community work ordered. It is a stark reminder of the consequences and is obviously designed to push home the message. However, I have discovered that there is perhaps a lesser regard for the perils of drink driving in New Zealand than in the UK and more people seem prepared to take the risk. Perhaps this can be put down to the limitations of the public transport system at certain times of the day, a lack of taxis in some areas, or maybe the 'I'm allowed two drinks before I am over the limit' mentality.

Eyesight regulations

Taking an eyesight test is a mandatory part of any licence application. The LTSA maintains that good vision is essential for road safety and if you can't see properly, you can't drive safely – makes sense really. Statistics show that a one to fourteen ratio of drivers have a vision defect, which may affect driving performance, but this factor does not apply solely to older drivers. Studies have shown that the highest number of people with bad eyesight are aged between 15 and 30, and 71 to 80 years old.

A formal eye test is not mandatory in the UK, unless reading the number plate of a car at a short distance can be construed as formal. Your eyesight will be tested in New Zealand whether you are a new driver or converting your full UK licence. The test is done using a machine at a licensing centre, but should you not pass the test, an eyesight certificate from a qualified optometrist must be produced. If you wear glasses or contact lenses at the eyesight screening check, your licence will reflect that by law you must wear them whenever you are driving.

BUYING A CAR

The car culture in New Zealand is such that there seems to be a virtually unlimited choice of vehicles available at car dealers on nearly every street corner in the main towns and cities. All vehicles are imported, some as brand new and others that have been first registered abroad – primarily in Japan.

A vehicle that has been registered overseas will in effect be used, and there is a legal requirement to display the date of registration and kilometres travelled on the sales notice. There have been reported cases of vehicles leaving Japan with, for example, 75,000 km on the clock and then arriving at the car sales depot with 35,000 km displayed. This is not a widespread practice, but perhaps the 'buyer beware' warning from the house buying section should be equally applied to the purchase of a vehicle.

Used cars in New Zealand are very much cheaper than in the UK and the quality of vehicles on offer is probably higher in relation to the purchase price. Our first car was a Toyota Camry 2.2 with only 11,000 km on the clock, costing less than $10,500. Dealers are keen to gain your business and are very amenable to striking a bargain with a potential purchaser. On this basis you should push hard for a generous discount, especially as a cash buyer – we actually paid $1500 less than the advertised price of our Camry.

INSURANCE

Car insurance in New Zealand is very cheap, although there are similar trends to the UK in that young drivers under the age of 25 will pay a high premium for a sports car or 'hot hatch', but only if they can find a company to cover them at all.

However, it is a staggering fact that car insurance is not compulsory in New Zealand, so there is no requirement to have a valid policy in order to keep or drive a car on the road.

What this effectively means is that a 15-year-old driver who holds a restricted licence can legally buy a high-performance car on the same day the licence is issued and drive it on public roads. The vehicle only has to be registered (taxed) and display a current Warrant of Fitness sticker, equivalent to the UK MOT test.

In the event of an accident involving an uninsured driver who is deemed to be at fault, there is very little option but to pursue recovery of the repair bill through the courts. However, if the 15-year-old uninsured driver's car is deemed a write-off and the owner has bought his flashy, I-want-to-impress-the-girls-and-be-part-of-the-in-crowd sports car on HP, the credit company will want to claim their stake first. Inevitably, this will leave the innocent party to foot the repair bill of his or her own vehicle that, if carried out under their own insurance policy, will almost certainly result in the loss of a no-claims bonus.

The bottom line is that no one can realistically be without insurance these days, as it provides a large degree of protection over and above the tragedy of an accident. The main reason that car policies are so cheap is because taking them out is entirely optional and, if the insurance companies want the business, they cannot afford to price themselves out of the market.

DRIVING IN NEW ZEALAND

The opening part of this chapter mentioned 'aggressive' drivers, but of course that does not apply to everybody and in general, driving around the country is an enjoyable experience. Many roads in towns and cities are built in long, straight lines, very similar in style to the USA, and are probably twice the width of those in the UK, with plenty of parking space on either side.

The speed limit in urban areas is 50 kph and is rigidly enforced by the police if they trap someone exceeding the limit. There is a 'zero tolerance' approach to driving offences and speeding tends to catch the eye of the law more frequently, as the irresponsible drivers push the boundaries to the limit in order to show off their latest customised creations. However, just as speed cameras in the UK are considered no more than a moneymaking venture, there is a similar opinion in New Zealand.

New Zealand roads

The major roads that cross the country are known as State Highways, with varying speed limits up to a maximum of 100 kph. However, in no way can they be compared to UK motorways, with the exception of some short stretches on the approaches to Auckland. About 90 per cent of the highways are no better than an average 'A' road in the UK, but with very few, if any, dual carriageways. Passing lanes have been built in some places where slow traffic has been taken into consideration to allow for steady flow. Many roads cross steep hills and mountains ranges, so tend to be naturally regulated by the land contours, although this does not deter the most dedicated speedster who firmly believes that he or she is entirely capable of becoming an F1 driver. Winding through valleys and clinging to the edge of mountains is common and can be a somewhat unnerving experience for a driver lacking in confidence.

There are very few, if any, entry or exit lanes from the State Highways, so the flow of traffic is interrupted with regular monotony by traffic lights at road intersections or rail crossings. It is precisely because of this, and the nature of the terrain, that the relatively 'short' drive in UK terms of only 658 km (300 miles) from Wellington to Auckland takes at least eight hours and is physically tiring. Automatic transmission vehicles seem to be the preference, as they take less effort to drive than a manual, and they suit the overall road conditions.

Vehicles are right-hand drive and all driving is on the left side of the road, as in the UK. Recent law has been introduced where drivers are required to indicate on a roundabout to clearly show which exit they intend to take. This is in line with the UK Highway Code, as is everything else, but there is one peculiar exception that takes a while to get acquainted with. If you are intending to turn left and another vehicle coming from the opposite direction is turning right into the same exit, then you are required by law to give way. If, however, there are two lanes of traffic on your side of the road, i.e. one lane to turn left and one for straight ahead, you may turn left if the traffic in the lane outside you is moving ahead. It may seem a strange rule, but in fact it does keep the flow of traffic moving, and works very well in most cases except when the impatient road hog exploits the smallest gap in the oncoming traffic and cuts in front of you to exercise the right of passage in accordance with the code.

Petrol stations are not as widespread in rural areas as they are in the UK, and fuel consumption is generally higher on longer journeys due to the stop-start nature of driving and more frequent gear changing because of the varying terrain. Awareness of the fuel capacity and consumption of your vehicle will be useful when travelling longer distances. Carrying an emergency, full fuel can in the boot is a sensible idea.

KIWI DRIVERS

If there is one word that sums up a large majority of drivers it has to be impatient. Tailgating is a very common occurrence and is regularly practised by those drivers who speed while regarding your driving at exactly the speed limit to be entirely unreasonable. They will take extraordinary risks to overtake one or two cars, although you will probably pass them again at the next set of lights while they are waiting to turn off at an intersection.

The Road Code states that if a vehicle is gaining on you then you should endeavour to keep as close to the left hand side of the road as possible and allow them to pass. Again, this is a reasonable law, but it was intended for drivers of slower moving vehicles – tractors, cars towing caravans or trailers – to make use of the 'hard shoulder' and allow the build up of traffic behind to dissipate. There are documented cases of police issuing a traffic offence ticket to drivers who plod along at 65 kph without any consideration for those vehicles following by *not* keeping into the left.

Another common practice is 'undertaking' on dual-lane highways. The drivers who persist in this extremely dangerous manoeuvre do not seem to care about the potentially fatal consequences to either themselves or others although, amazingly, this practice is not considered illegal. All cars are fitted with indicators, but an incredible number appear to be either defective or the driver has no idea of how, or inclination, to use them; regretfully, I strongly suspect it is mostly the latter!

Whilst this perhaps paints a grim picture, it must be stressed that if you have your wits about you, drive within both the speed limit and the limitations of your car and follow the Road Code you will not fall foul of the law. The tearaways will ultimately be caught out and quite often learn their lesson the hard way.

In the first edition of this book I mentioned that calls were once again being made for a review of the licensing structure in New Zealand to try to eliminate the growing problem of irresponsible young drivers. That debate is still very much ongoing some three years later with no changes enforced so far, but an increase in young driver-related fatalities appears to have raised the issue to a much greater level than perhaps has been witnessed for some considerable time.

13
General Information

This section will provide useful snippets of information that may help you to prepare for arrival in New Zealand.

CLIMATE AND WEATHER

The seasons in New Zealand are exactly the opposite of those in the UK. Celebrating Christmas in the garden wearing shorts, t-shirt and sunglasses is something that still feels quite strange, especially when you serve the traditional roast turkey with all the trimmings on Christmas Day!

Depending on where you live in New Zealand will obviously determine the climate to expect. The country was named by early Maori as Aotearoa, which translates as 'land of the long white cloud'. This was for the simple reason that the mountainous peaks that stretch from north to south are often shrouded in cloud due to the diverse climate changes.

New Zealand lies in the path of prevailing westerly winds, producing contrasts in temperature and rainfall on either side of the South Island Alps, and the continuous backbone of primarily bush land ranges dividing the North Island. The rainforests on the western coast of the South Island have been known to be swamped with up to seven metres (that's over 22 feet!) of rainfall a year, yet the Canterbury plains on the eastern coast are relatively dry and warm, occasionally suffering from drought conditions. The difference is less dramatic in the North Island, but the further north you go, the more sub-tropical the climate becomes.

Despite its somewhat isolated position in the Southern Pacific Ocean, the country has a generally mild, maritime climate that can often be wet, overcast and unpredictable, as well as warm, sunny and dry. Two main geographical features – the mountains and the sea – dominate and affect the weather patterns across the country.

Most areas of New Zealand have between 63 and 165 cms of rainfall spread throughout the year. Mean annual temperatures range from 10°C in the south to 16°C in the north with the coldest months being July through to September and the warmest January and February. Temperatures in the summer months can reach 35°C in sheltered spots.

There is a very well documented phenomenon in New Zealand – the hole in the ozone layer that sits above the country. The result of this is a higher than average UV index, further accentuated by the cleaner air, which increases the burn time. Many schools have a policy during summer months for their pupils to wear sun hats during break times for protection.

It is said that elements of all four seasons can be experienced during just one day in some parts of New Zealand and, with such a diverse weather system, that should not come as too much of a surprise.

EARTHQUAKES

New Zealand is not nicknamed the 'shaky' islands for nothing. Minor earthquakes are a regular occurrence. If you have never experienced the real thing before then you should be prepared, as it can of course be quite disturbing.

The country ranks amongst one of the most active seismic places on earth due to its geographical location on the boundary of the Pacific and Australian tectonic plates. In the easterly region of the North Island the Pacific plate is being forced under the Australian plate, but under the South Island, the two plates push past each other sideways. This tectonic activity, as we experience it today, started in New Zealand over 25 million years ago, so it is nothing new. Earthquakes and other seismic activity result from the movement of the earth's crust along such active faults, although a majority are not strong enough to be widely felt.

New Zealand has a widespread network of seismic monitors and equipment that record about 14,000 earthquakes a year. Of these, about 100–150 are big enough to be felt and have the potential to cause minor damage in some cases. In our first year of living in the country, three earthquakes ranging from 4.6 to 5.4 on the Richter Scale left a few minor cracks in our newly laid concrete driveway, but the only sign inside the house has been the odd crooked picture.

Advice received before we left the UK was to ensure that shelves in cupboards containing glass and crystal items were lined with bubble wrap, but we decided that this would look particularly unsightly. We have however bought a tub of the appropriately named Earthquake Wax, that is similar to Blu Tack but more durable, and both recommended and used by museums to protect their artefacts.

The earthquakes we have experienced so far have had very different characteristics. They can range from one small jolt similar to the intensity of your car rolling into a tree at about 2 kph, through to physical shaking for a few seconds preceded by a rumble, similar to a train approaching. The ripples spreading through the earth from the epicentre, and eventually arriving in your area in the same way as ripples on water arrive at the shoreline, cause this particular effect.

Having to cope with earthquakes is a fact of life in New Zealand and you simply have to accept that they will occur. Insurance is a wonderful commodity and buildings insurance is calculated on the rebuilding cost of the total floor area of your property including outhouses.

Accurately predicting what would be classed as a significant event is impossible, which is why house owners are obliged to take out earthquake insurance.

A government organisation known as the Earthquake Commission (EQC) provides insurance for natural disaster damage to your home, personal possessions and land. Buildings are covered up to a maximum of $100,000 and personal effects are insured up to $20,000. Cover is obtained automatically when you take out a home or contents policy. There are certain limitations to this scheme – the EQC pays the value of damaged land at the time of the earthquake or natural disaster, or the repair cost, whichever is lower, for example – but it is comforting that the New Zealand government recognises the need to provide for additional funding in such an earthquake-prone country.

TELEVISION AND RADIO

There are five 'free to air' television channels in New Zealand, but the one major difference is the lack of a licence fee in New Zealand, so complaints about programme quality and scheduling are almost unheard of.

Mountainous ranges and surrounding hills mean that some areas are not covered by normal terrestrial signals which rely on line of sight between the aerial on your roof and the transmitter. Even in some suburbs of built-up areas where you would reasonably expect good reception, houses are 'blind' and have no choice but to subscribe to SKY or cable television. The satellite service in New Zealand does not offer as much programme choice as the UK does and viewing can still be disrupted by atmospheric conditions such as heavy rain, which can be frequent at particular times of the year depending on where you live.

Subscription packages to SKY vary, but the sports channels in particular will at times broadcast an event that is being transmitted on free to air TV at the same time. Being a rugby mad nation there is also a dedicated rugby channel available via SKY, but much of its broadcasting time features reruns of recent matches from the past and present season, together with the occasional vintage game showing the all-conquering All Blacks in another stunning victory. However, this is the only channel where you will get coverage of Northern hemisphere events such as the Six Nations and domestic league and cup competitions, so if you are a die-hard rugby fan and intend keeping up with the UK scene, you will need the Rugby Channel. The cost of a complete SKY package amounts to about $80 per month so is similar in many respects to the UK.

As in most countries across the world, radio stations are fairly wide ranging although there is probably less choice given the relatively small population. The same problem with terrain affects radio broadcasts, and is more noticeable and frequent whilst driving.

There are broadcasting standards applied to both television and radio, but it should be noted that these appear to be much more liberal than those enforced in the UK. The use of what may be construed as less than courteous language is quite common, yet appears to be generally accepted by the viewing and listening public. Programmes are graded for viewing in the same way as they are in the UK and although the watershed is supposed to be set at 8.30pm, it appears to be non-existent at times.

ENTERTAINMENT

The country is very much taken by the outdoor way of life. How adventurous you are will determine how you spend your leisure time.

There is a good choice of cinemas both multi and single screen in the main cities showing the latest films, plus ten-pin bowling, go-karting and swimming. Indoor climbing walls seem quite popular, but netball, basketball, rounders, cricket, soccer, golf and of course rugby have strong followers from both the young and older communities.

Listing all the things to do would take forever and why should I spoil your fun in exploring for yourself?

BARS AND PUBS

There is a very good selection of hostelries all in competition for trade, both regular and passing. Most have a huge screen TV to cater for sports events, in particular rugby matches featuring the All Blacks and Super 14 teams. Bars in central locations of major cities will be more expensive, especially if they are promoting a certain theme. Irish-style pubs serving beers such as Guinness and Kilkenny together with a fairly large range of whiskies are popular, while only a few doors away may be a bar stocked entirely with beers from Holland or Belgium.

A majority of pubs and bars will also promote their range of poker machines, commonly known as pokies. These are basically electronic 'one-armed bandits' where the money raised is not counted as pub profits but ploughed back into the community. Most pubs are limited to nine of these machines, but they are generally linked to a central jackpot accumulator that is by law not permitted to exceed about $1,000 before it must be won. They are capable of accepting $5, $10 and $20 notes as well as $2 coins and the choice of how much you wish to stake on each spin of the reels is entirely up to the player, although the top limit is restricted to just under $2.50. In a majority of places, there is at least a one in nine chance of winning the jackpot. Some clubs and larger pubs have 18 machines, others up to 30 and the casinos have hundreds, so the odds of winning anything that could be classed as major increases exponentially.

Horse and dog racing is a huge industry and self-service betting terminals – known as the Totaliser Agency Betting or TAB – are available in many clubs and bars. Racing is broadcast on its own exclusive television channel and can feature live events from early morning until late evening, including those beamed from Australia.

EATING OUT

New Zealand is a fantastic place for lovers of good food and drink. This is almost certainly attributable to its abundance of fresh produce and renowned wine industry.

The range of top quality, local produce on offer includes lamb, beef, pork, venison, mussels, crayfish, whitebait, scallops, salmon, a huge selection of deep-sea fish and of course, the famous Bluff oysters.

New Zealand chefs are largely influenced by Pacific, European and Asian cuisines to prepare superb meals with the freshest meat, fish and vegetables available. Not surprisingly, with so many sheep in the country, lamb is a principal food source and Canterbury lamb is world-renowned, usually served as a roast dinner. Pumpkin and kumara (sweet potato) are very popular vegetables and are used to complement meals in much the same way as swede and potatoes are in the UK. Pumpkin soup is a favourite but it is an acquired taste for some.

Seafood is available all year round in New Zealand, where no one lives more than two hours' drive from the sea. Local speciality dishes of fish, crayfish or shellfish are advertised across the country and offered at a very reasonable price in comparison with the UK market. Popular ocean fish includes snapper, terakihi, hoki, orange roughy and John Dory. Fresh water fish such as trout and salmon are caught under a personal fishing licence and some hotels, generally those located on renowned fishing lakes and rivers, will even cook your catch for you. Trout are not sold commercially in order to safeguard the river stocks.

The New Zealand dairy industry is world famous for high quality products including butter, cheese, fresh milk, yoghurt, cream and ice cream. Fruit is grown in abundance and supermarkets have a large choice of oranges, apples, pears, peaches, apricots and plums. Kiwi fruit is of course available all over the country and, in fact, New Zealand accounts for over 30 per cent of the world's kiwi fruit exports. However, you may not know that the fruit is a native of China and was called the Chinese gooseberry or monkey's peach. It was introduced to New Zealand in 1904 but did not have its name changed to kiwi fruit until 1959.

A three-course meal can vary in price from about $40 right up to $150 or more depending on where you choose to eat. Some buffet restaurants will offer a soup, carvery and dessert for as little as $15 and are good value for money although the food is, quite reasonably, of a more basic quality. Many are licensed as BYO (bring your own) establishments where a small corkage charge may be made for wine you take along, but in a vast majority of cases, BYO applies to wine only. Tipping is not expected but is of course welcome for exceptional service.

Dining is normally *à la carte* in a relaxed, informal atmosphere, but there is also a wide choice of cafés, brasseries and bistros providing excellent, moderately priced snack meals along with wine, beer and spirits. International food halls in main shopping centres are also popular, offering a wide variety of freshly cooked 'fast-food' at very reasonable prices. 'Fish and chips' is considered to be a Friday night tradition in New Zealand and shops are plentiful, but everything is cooked to order rather than sitting in warming cabinets until someone buys it; I can guarantee that you will appreciate the difference in quality, although there is still something to be said for tasting British-style fish and chips when back in the UK on our holidays.

There are over 400 vineyards in a country well served by a maritime climate and long growing season, ideal conditions for the cultivation of grapes. The selection of wines available both in supermarkets and restaurants is huge and New Zealand produces world-class examples of sauvignon blanc, chardonnay, merlot and pinot noir as mainstream brands. Australian wines are also extremely well represented and there is a very small selection of German and Spanish wines on offer in some liquor stores, although they are not particularly common in supermarkets.

A Maori style feast is known as a *hangi* where meat, often a whole wild pig, and vegetables are steam cooked in an underground oven. In areas of natural volcanic activity pools of natural boiling water are used for cooking and the sulphur content does not taint the food. Working villages in and around Rotorua are particularly popular for this type of eating, and tourists can witness and sample naturally cooked items such as corn-on-the-cob for a very modest donation.

14

Major Cities and Regions

Earlier in the book I mentioned how work and jobs are determined by regional trends, so it is perhaps helpful to include a very brief regional outline of New Zealand to assist with your decision-making. The idea is to provide you with an extremely brief picture of the country as a whole, but primarily to highlight industries in relation to potential business and work opportunities. Reproducing page after page of information that can be found in any good fact book was never the intention. Once again, it is strongly recommended that you conduct much more research on a particular district before making any sort of decision based solely on the information contained in this book!

There is a longer feature about Wellington because of its status as the capital city.

The location of each region or place can be found on the map on page 3.

NORTHLAND

Hailed as the warmest region of New Zealand, Northland is listed as an area of outstanding beauty and expanding economic growth. The region has a population of about 140,000 who inhabit widespread towns, cities and communities throughout the urban and rural land area of some 7,800 square kilometres.

Northland is considered the sub-tropical part of the country and enjoys warm, humid summers when average temperatures range from 22°C to 26°C. During the winter months highs of between 14°C and 17°C are quite normal. Historically it is where New Zealand's first people landed and was home to eighteenth century European settlers from Britain, Ireland and France – they must have found the golden beaches and bush-clad forestry very much to their liking!

The west coast is rugged, while the east is renowned for its beaches and water sports in support of the tourist sector; some of the best sub-aqua diving can be found off the Northland coast.

Northland is deemed a region of significant commercial potential. Established industries include dairy farming, forestry, horticulture, wood processing, fruit growing, fishing, boat building, cement mining and tourism. Major companies in the retail market are well represented throughout the region, but family owned businesses are widespread and include cheese making, jewellery, clothing and skin care products.

A relatively new deep-water port has been established just south of the city of Whangarei at Marsden Point that can only boost the regional employment figures as it becomes more developed.

Northland is renowned for its contribution to the contemporary arts scene and is a popular destination for travellers who come for the year-round festivals, events and performances.

AUCKLAND

Nearly three-quarters of the land area occupied by the Auckland region consists of islands in the Hauraki Gulf, yet it still has a population of some 1.3 million. That is more than double the number who live in the Wellington region and is made up largely of Maori, European, Asian and Polynesian people, which ensure its reputation as a thriving cosmopolitan society and culture.

Some 70 per cent of all overseas migrants choose to settle in the Auckland region and it is recognised as the world's largest 'Polynesian' city. Around

64 per cent of its residents are of European descent – Britain, Holland, Yugoslavia and Hungary are well represented – with the remainder made up of about 13 per cent Pacific Islanders, 11 per cent Maori and a growing Asian community currently standing at 12 per cent.

Despite its size, infrastructure and accessibility – the country's main international airport is located in the southern suburbs of the city – it is not the capital of New Zealand, despite the belief that many inhabitants think it should be.

Built on 48 extinct volcano cones, many of which are now parks and recreation spaces, and boasting three natural and spectacular harbours, Auckland uses these assets to its best advantage in attracting visitors to the city. There is so much to explore both outside and within the main city area including white sandy beaches, award winning parks, rainforest, wineries and more than 50 'South Pacific' islands. Auckland is named the 'City of Sails' as there are rumoured to be more yachts per capita than any other city in the world, as well as it being home of the Americas Cup challenges. Naturally, one of the best ways of appreciating the area is from on the water and every conceivable type of boat can be chartered from many locations around the region, including Americas Cup style yachts.

Auckland enjoys a warm coastal climate where the average summer temperature is about 24°C, and between 12°C and 15°C in winter. Rainfall amounts to about 120 cms per year. The weather in Auckland can be notoriously changeable, however, and the 'four seasons in one day' experience is not unknown!

Major industries include technology – both bio and information – film production, engineering and the food and beverage trade. Manufacturing accounts for 40 per cent of the country's output and about 45 per cent of wholesalers, responsible for New Zealand-wide distribution, are based here. Many worldwide operators have their head offices and operations located in Auckland, including fast food firms, insurance and financial institutions to name but a few.

Like most major conurbations, traffic congestion is recognised as a real problem although Auckland appears to suffer more than most. There are major studies underway to try and improve the road system, but be prepared for some delays in and around the city and allow a little extra time to get around. Despite its size there is no underground rail system in Auckland or indeed anywhere else in New Zealand, which is probably due to the country being prone to earthquakes and the associated risks being too great.

Dining out and entertainment opportunities in Auckland are seemingly endless and the city has taken on a style of cuisine known as 'Pacific Rim'. This is due to the influences and blending of Asian and Pacific flavours and almost dominates the restaurant scene, numbering over 900 at the last count! There are 80-plus vineyards in the Auckland region, many of which produce award-winning wine. North of the city is the cheese-making district located in the Puhoi Valley and, like much of New Zealand, seafood is a prominent feature on just about every menu.

Auckland is growing in stature and popularity as a destination for those seeking further education. It attracts a very wide range of students from around the world, who are well catered for in terms of learning institutions.

It is the cosmopolitan style and opportunities to participate in a huge variety of outdoor activities that makes Auckland a popular destination for world travellers and prospective migrants alike.

WAIKATO

The Waikato district is known for its dairy and farming industry, and the city of Hamilton is a major service centre for this expansive and fertile agricultural region.

New Zealand's dairy industry is perhaps the biggest employer in the region and Hamilton has a well-established research and development capability employing modern technology and methods.

Regional industries include horse breeding, forestry and paper processing, fishing, horticulture and floriculture, very much related to its agricultural status.

Hamilton has a population of only 115,000 despite the University of Waikato and Waikato Polytechnic being located there.

The region has a similar climate to that of Auckland, although cooler temperatures will be found in the more mountainous areas to the south.

BAY OF PLENTY

An extremely popular region for New Zealanders and tourists alike, the Bay of Plenty has established itself at the forefront of a fast growing economy. The city of Tauranga is located on the coast and is the fifth largest in New Zealand, as well as being the largest export port in the country.

There are new and innovative business opportunities that will be of particular interest to those migrants under the business categories. The population is growing at a rate of five times the national average, which may be attributable to a local organisation called Priority One. They focus their attention on business and the economic growth of the region and have a well-earned reputation for matching business migrants to specific opportunities.

There are over 12,000 businesses located in the Bay of Plenty region that include manufacturing, engineering, logistics, tourism, research, health and construction. All of these industries experience occupational shortages in many disciplines including electricians, fitters and turners, welders, surveyors, carpenters, drivers, plumbers, nurses, doctors and social workers, to name but a few.

GISBORNE

The Gisborne district has a population of 44,000 of which 75 per cent live in Gisborne City. Just about half the population are of Maori descent.

Pastoral farming is the most important industry in the region, but there has been a steady rise in related industries such as horticulture and food processing. Grape production is a well-established business, with 17 wineries, one of which is the largest in the country. Gisborne is also known as the Chardonnay capital of New Zealand. Opportunities are also available in wood processing, printing and fishing.

Gisborne is the first city in the world to see the sunrise and the climate is very much one of long, warm summer days and mild winters. Top temperatures of 38°C have been recorded in summer and just over two months in every 12 will experience 24°C or more. Famed for its uncrowded beaches and vast tracts of wilderness, Gisborne is a favourite seaside destination for many.

Housing in the region is relatively low-priced in comparison with other areas and there is a good choice of educational institutions.

TARANAKI

The city of New Plymouth sits right on the western tip of Taranaki alongside the extinct volcanic cone of Mount Taranaki, also referred to as Mount Egmont. It is a mere 30-minute drive from the mountain environment to the sea and it is quite possible to be standing in snow on the peak of Taranaki in the morning and surfing off a beach at New Plymouth in the afternoon.

The region is renowned for its scenery, rainforest and parks and gardens, experiencing average temperatures of 14–25°C in summer and 6–16°C in winter.

The population of the whole district stands at a little over 100,000 and New Plymouth houses the largest percentage of people at 67,000. The influence of the region is very much European, reflected in the 90 per cent of those inhabitants who have descended from there.

Major industries include dairying, engineering, tourism, exports and petrochemicals. Over 60 per cent of farms in the region are dedicated to dairy production, while the oil and gas industries are responsible for contributing over $90 million per annum to the nation's economy.

HAWKES BAY

Long, sandy beaches and the capital of Napier – the art deco city of New Zealand – ensure that Hawkes Bay has much to offer both tourists and migrants.

There is always a demand for both skilled and semi-skilled labour to ensure that the food production sector maintains its reputation as one of the country's leaders. Positions such as fruit pickers, food processors, fork-lift drivers and packers are always open, although the overall growth in the region has resulted in a considerably lower unemployment rate than in other regions. Skilled labour is in high demand, especially from people with trade qualifications such as builders, plumbers, electricians and professional lines such as engineers.

The area features a relaxed and peaceful lifestyle and tourism is making its mark on the industrial front, probably due to the stable, warm climate that Hawkes Bay residents enjoy.

MANAWATU/WANGANUI

Recognised as the gateway of the North Island, Manawatu is a large region of diverse physical features. Outdoor activity is the name of the game here as you can spend days on the beach, in the mountains or exploring rivers and gorges.

A relatively small population of just over 100,000 live in this region, 75,000 of which are European. The city of Palmerston North is the sixth largest in New Zealand and other cities such as New Plymouth and Wellington are only two to three hours' drive away. Daily temperatures range from highs of 22°C to lows of 12°C and rainfall averages some 100 cms per year.

Major industries include pastoral and dairy farming, forestry, oil and gas production. It is also the home of Massey University, a major player in tertiary education.

WELLINGTON

Capital city and home to the government of New Zealand, Wellington is the southern-most capital in the world. The city is named after the first Duke of Wellington, who was also installed as the British Prime Minister from 1828 to 1830. It is also known as the windy city, because of its physical location within the 'roaring 40s' and the natural funnel effect caused by the end of the mountain ranges in the North Island and the start of the ranges in the South Island.

Wellington is a small city – it would fit comfortably into Central London – and at its widest point measures less than a mile. So exploration on foot is easy and it takes only 20 minutes to walk from one side of the city to the other. Sitting alongside a huge natural harbour and surrounded by rolling green hills, this magnificent setting helps to enhance the vibrant mix of arts and culture on offer that is unrivalled anywhere else in New Zealand.

Nearly all residents in Wellington live within 2.5 kilometres of the sea and enjoy the greatest proportion of open space per capita of any other city. In other words, it is not in the least bit crowded compared with other capitals around the world.

In a recent 'top city' one hundred poll conducted by *Condé Nast Traveller* Magazine, regarded by many travel writers as the ultimate in awards, Wellington polled eighteenth place, and was the only city in New Zealand to feature. People we have since met during their holiday to the region expressed a strong desire to stay, having visited Wellington.

So what makes the city so attractive to immigrants? It is hard to pin down one specific aspect, but perhaps the most significant is that Wellington could be compared to many towns and city centres up and down the length of the UK, but without the constant hustle and bustle that blights many places today. We have met tourists here who marvel at how clean and welcoming the place is, coupled with the abundance and range of shops, amenities and, of course, things to do.

Work and business opportunities

New Zealand has been awarded the title of best business environment in the world following a survey by World Bank and Wellington is recognised as the leading city in the country. The key to success in business is communications and Wellington has the envious status of being the only city in the world to operate four high-speed fibre optic networks. Naturally, this sort of technology attracts major market leaders in more diverse sectors, which only serves to enhance the reputation of 'standard' world players in insurance and finance and state-owned institutions. Industries such as tourism, manufacturing, software development and even film production – Peter Jackson of *Lord of the Rings* fame has his studios in Wellington – are rapidly expanding and all of them need a robust and innovative information technology system, yet another sector that always has lots of vacancies and sometimes struggles to keep up with demand. During the 2005 British and Irish Lions tour, recruitment agencies were actively posting notices and adverts at airports, petrol stations and even in toilets to tempt prospective migrants back to New Zealand on a permanent basis, an indication of just how short the capital is on IT experts and of the initiative shown by companies to target a potentially rich source of expertise.

There are tremendous opportunities opening up all the time in the research and development field, given their alignment with new and updated government policies. Subjects such as medicine, technology, engineering, water and atmosphere, animal health, geology and seismology, nuclear and environmental sciences all fall under the research and development umbrella.

Living in Wellington

The average rent for a modest three-bedroomed house is about £175 per week and the average price starts around £135,000, although as was mentioned in an earlier chapter, there are physically larger properties for your money available within commuting distance of the city. The whole Wellington region covers an approximate area of 3,200 square kilometres of the North Island and consists of five cities and districts, with a combined population of only 450,000. Greater London would fit into this area a little over five times, but has a population of over seven million – fifteen times as many people!

The city is well served by a wide choice of public and private schools, many of which offer boarding facilities. The options for tertiary education are numerous and cater for virtually anything from apprenticeships to on-job training, to degree courses in academic subjects.

Attractions and recreation

The opportunities to indulge in a huge variety of outdoor activities are almost endless in a region of natural amenities. There are about 160 kilometres of designated tracks and walkways through natural reserve land surrounding the city alone and most are accessible by foot from the centre of the city. Surfing, scuba diving, sailing, kayaking and mountain biking are all extremely popular pastimes due to the temperate climate, which means you can be outdoors just about all year round.

During the summer months there are events that take place around the waterfront and on the beach at Oriental Parade which attract visitors from far and wide. There are some beautiful beaches on the other side of the harbour, around Eastbourne, that are perfect for family recreation and can be reached by road in about 20 minutes from the city centre or by ferry across the harbour.

The city is home to Te Papa, New Zealand's national museum located on the waterfront in a building designed to withstand earthquake damage. The whole structure 'sits' on rubber mounts visible in a special gallery just outside the museum entrance. Interactive features abound inside and the history of New Zealand can be traced from the Awesome Forces feature that covers the 'making' of the country right through to the Maori settlers and European immigrants. What makes Te Papa special is that there is no entry charge other than for some occasional exhibitions and the whole place, coupled with the dedicated and friendly staff, is designed to make you feel extremely welcome.

There are of course other museums and galleries throughout the city and indeed the Wellington region, each offering its own unique look at aspects of life in New Zealand.

Eating, drinking and entertainment

Wellington is renowned for its range and choice when it comes to eating out and entertainment. Restaurants and cafés are everywhere and you are spoilt for which one to pick. I sometimes wonder just how some of them manage to stay in business given the competition that surrounds them. Indian, Chinese, Japanese, Turkish, Italian, Mexican and American style restaurants are all featured and are of a good standard, an absolute must if they are to succeed.

There are pubs that sell imported UK beers – Tetley, Newcastle Brown, London Pride, Brains, Boddingtons to name but a few – and others that are totally European, focused on selling Belgian and Dutch brews.

Cinemas are of the multi-screen type and even feature luxury lounges where you can sit in reclining armchairs and have a meal served at your side-table during the film, a wonderful experience especially during a three-hour epic. There is a very vibrant and modern club scene in Wellington that caters for all types of music ranging from current trends to jazz. For the party people, clubbing through the night at the weekend is very much an option!

One individual who returned to Wellington after working abroad for some years reinforced the point of just how good life in the city is by saying:

> Wellington has everything great that a big city has but is relatively small. Traffic outside the rush hour is a breeze, people are friendly and there are loads of exciting things to do.

Nothing more really needs to be said except that Wellington will not disappoint!

(With grateful thanks to Wellington City Council for their valuable input.)

MARLBOROUGH

The main urban centres in Marlborough are Blenheim and Picton, which is where the Cook Strait ferry from Wellington terminates.

Tourism, pastoral farming, wine making, forestry and aviation are classed as the major industries associated with the region. Marlborough wines are recognised as some of the best in the world and production accounts for over 50 per cent of New Zealand's wine exports.

The district is blessed with excellent flying conditions and a relative lack of air traffic, and has been synonymous with aeronautical training and maintenance since 1939. The New Zealand Air Force has a base at Woodbourne, which is also the home of SafeAir, a successful aviation provider and location of the largest propeller maintenance works in the Asia/Pacific region. The business has four main product lines –

maintenance, repair, overhaul and modification for a range of airframes including helicopters, engines and avionic components.

Marlborough is fast developing into a desirable area, housing a broad range of businesses and can boast the lowest unemployment rate in New Zealand. However, the lack of skilled labour in some disciplines could be considered a constraint at times. Having said that, there are employment opportunities in most occupational categories, including support industries such as health and education.

The climate is a mix of sub-alpine and sub-tropical. The average annual rainfall in this small district can vary from 60 cms in the east to around 200 cms in the west!

TASMAN

Covering about 3,000 square kilometres, Tasman is a diverse region of mountains, rivers, valleys, plains and a coastline that provides superb recreational facilities for just about any outdoor pursuit.

Major attractions are the Abel Tasman and Kahurangi National Parks, and Waikoropupu Springs, said to produce the cleanest water in the world.

A majority of people living in Tasman work in farming, forestry, fishing and tourism so, with the focus on quality exports, there are businesses to service this need. The region is recognised as having the most working artists and crafts related people in New Zealand.

Tasman has become a popular place to retire, with many old folk electing to spend their remaining time in populated areas such as Richmond and Golden Bay.

The population of about 41,000 is made up of over 90 per cent European and 7 per cent Maori.

WEST COAST

The West Coast stretches along some 450 km of rocky and rugged coastline. It is home to a similar mix of European and Maori people as Tasman but totalling about 25 per cent less.

Given the rocky nature of the whole region, there is a lack of arable land for crop growing, although dairy farming is a key industry because of the lush grazing in many places. There are rich deposits of coal and gold that were discovered by the Europeans in the mid 1800s, which is why mining has been the centre of the economy throughout the West Coast ever since.

The region is somewhat isolated from the rest of the South Island as it is protected by the alpine mountain ranges stretching down the centre of the island. There are only four passes available through the mountains resulting in an independent community. Many say that the West Coast is how New Zealand used to be.

Employment opportunities are many, because the service and retail sectors, as secondary trades to mining, suffer a general shortage of skilled workers. Qualified people are especially sought after to meet the growing demand for construction of new housing and commercial premises, as well as all those spin-off trades needed to support the industry.

The region is subjected to the second highest rainfall in the country, averaging about 23 cms in each of the four seasons, accounting for the lush pasture! Mountains, rivers, rainforests and wilderness contribute to the feeling of remoteness, but the West Coast does not lag behind the times because of it.

CANTERBURY

Over half a million people live in Canterbury province and 65 per cent of those live in the city of Christchurch, where they enjoy a pleasant climate and all four seasons are distinctly defined.

The Southern Alps separates the region from the rocky West Coast and the contrast could not be more dramatic. Superb natural harbours and sandy beaches along the Pacific shoreline are a major attraction for both business and tourism alike.

With such a large number of people, by general New Zealand standards, concentrated in one city, Christchurch has much to offer the potential migrant. Innovative businesses and knowledge-based industries form the backbone of its success, but the city is also noted for its education and research facilities. Recent statistics show that over the past seven years, some 33 per cent of the jobs created in New Zealand have come out of the Canterbury region.

The city covers a large area, effectively negating significant traffic problems that would normally be associated with smaller, more compact cities. It is very much influenced by English culture; you can hire a punt on the River Avon that flows through the middle of the city and many of the buildings would not appear out of place in the middle of Bath! Christchurch is also the staging post for support to the Antarctic survey missions.

Major industries located across the region include engineering, agriculture, food processing, fishing, construction, forestry, manufacturing and electronics.

The Canterbury plains are a fertile, arable area where just about anything will grow despite the region having the lowest average rainfall in the whole of New Zealand. The average temperatures range from 10°C in winter to highs of 24°C in summer.

There are many attractions throughout the region, ranging from whale watching off Kaikoura, bathing in thermal pools at Hanmer Springs and enjoying the breathtaking scenery of the Banks Peninsula, all contributing to a lively flow of migrants and tourists.

OTAGO

The city of Dunedin is known as the gateway to Otago and also has the nickname of 'University City'. The overall population is a little over 120,000 but of these, some 20 per cent are in tertiary student education. This would perhaps account for its multicultural composition of European, Maori, Asian and Pacific Island ethnicities.

Dunedin is a mix of Edwardian and Victorian architecture housing a wide variety of shops, restaurants, cafés, galleries, museums and theatres. The average price of housing is generally lower than other parts of the country further north and the rental market is well served to house the student numbers.

The average summer temperature is about 19°C, dropping to around 9°C during daylight hours in the winter.

Otago spans a region of diverse landscapes, from the white sandy beaches on the Pacific Coast to the ski-fields of the Southern Alps a few hours' drive away. The opportunity for outdoor sports and activities are almost endless. There are award winning nature reserves on the edge of Otago Harbour, and within a short distance of Dunedin city centre you can visit the only mainland breeding place of the royal albatross and see a colony of yellow-eyed penguins, the rarest in the world. The many coastal walks and beaches will reveal a wide range of wildlife, particularly seals, in their natural habitat.

The region, like many others, continues to experience skill shortages in specific areas such as engineering, health care, teaching and chefs. There are other opportunities in the retail and service sectors to support the demand from those in tertiary education. Key industries are agriculture, fashion, forestry, horticulture, biotechnology and engineering.

SOUTHLAND

The most southerly province in New Zealand – next stop is Antarctica – Southland is a mix of Celtic and Maori influences despite over 92 per cent of the ethnic composition being European.

Of the 93,000 people living in the Southland region, over 25 per cent are involved in manufacturing. Engineering firms are widespread, and turn out products and services to support major industries such as farming, wine growing and transport. Health, agriculture and tourism account for the other main employment opportunities. Arable farmland produces a variety of crops and the sheep, beef and dairy industries are all well established. Around the coast, fishermen catch crayfish, cod and oysters that are of superb quality given the unpolluted waters fed by the Southern Ocean.

In comparison with other cities further north, the capital of Invercargill and other regional towns do not suffer any real traffic problems because of the wide roads and relatively small populace.

The pace of life in Southland is renowned for being as slow or fast as you wish to make it and the outdoor recreation scene is a key factor that drives people to settle there. Add to that the lowest median house prices in New Zealand, and it is easy to see why some migrants aim for Southland from the outset as a place where they can get away from the hustle and bustle of city life.

SLOW

PENGUINS
CROSSING

15

Final Thoughts

At the beginning of this book, I said that the whole logistical and mental challenge of moving to New Zealand was not an easy one and never has a truer word been said. What you may be asking yourself now is exactly how we feel almost seven years on after deciding to emigrate and making New Zealand our home. The simple answer is that we have no regrets at all.

Everyone will experience different emotions and reactions, especially with regard to family. We have met people here who accept and cope with these particular issues in exactly the same way that we have. Others may struggle to adjust to their new life because they either cannot or will not distance themselves from continually making comparisons with what was left behind in the UK. Whichever way you look at it, the move has been made and returning to the UK on a permanent basis for whatever reason could result in some complicated financial problems.

Effectively, if you were to return, it would probably mean a new start back in the UK where the average cost of even a three-bedroomed house on a densely populated estate is probably double what it is in New Zealand. Unless you have access to a large sum of reserve money, or a well-paid job to walk back into should you decide to retrace your steps, be clear that the New Zealand dollar would not go very far in the UK. Of course, if you are extremely unhappy with life in New Zealand then returning to the UK will no doubt be of great comfort, but it is worth making the point about housing and money in particular.

With the exchange rate averaging around $2.50 to the pound, then the reality is that your $350,000 house in New Zealand is worth about

£140,000 on the UK market. I have not even looked into matters of capital gains tax but that is another potential cost to be reckoned with should it be applicable. Account for the cost of moving everything you own and flights back to the UK and there might be enough money left to buy a small starter home, which could be a far cry from what you probably lived in before you emigrated and certainly nothing like what you would have enjoyed in New Zealand.

There are so many other aspects to look into if you take the option to relocate back to Britain. How about the new TVs, washing machine and tumble dryer for instance? Will they be suitable for use in the UK? Will they have spares support? Will you have to buy new again? So many questions, most of which I simply would not want to contemplate!

Our decision to move to the other side of the world was made on the strength that once we had left, there would be no intention of going back and we would simply have to work through any problems that cropped up along the way.

This approach was always centred on our desire to experience more than continuing to eke out an existence in a country of seemingly endless taxation and ever-increasing cost of living. Couple this with over population, and you will be able to comprehend what sparked the catalyst for our life-changing move. This mindset does not necessarily apply to everyone and only 12 months after publishing the first edition of this book, our son decided that New Zealand did not provide his type of lifestyle. He returned to live and work in London to follow his ambitions of a music career where his success is accompanied by enjoyment of the hustle and bustle in the 'big smoke'.

For us, the move to New Zealand has brought greater rewards than we could ever have expected in terms of the lifestyle, country and people. Modern, efficient air transport means that our roots are still only 24 hours' travel away. With the telecommunications companies all vying for business and especially use of the internet, chatting with family and friends is both cheap and easy, although I acknowledge that this isn't the same as being physically in their presence.

Nobody can make such a life changing decision based solely on reading one book and no matter how wonderful the portrayal of any country may be, everyone's personal circumstances are unique. For the record, we had never been to New Zealand before we actually emigrated and everything we 'discovered' about the country came from reading, internet research, DVD/video tapes and talking with people who had been there. Initially, friends and family were not slow in doubting our sanity or reasons for wanting to leave the UK without first visiting New Zealand, but we only committed ourselves after a great deal of discussion, deliberation and even arguments in many circles. We remain convinced that there was a degree of jealousy about what we were about to achieve. We lost count of the number of people who asked if there was room in a suitcase for them!

If after reading this you are seriously contemplating the biggest move of your life, to take up residency in such a beautiful, clean country, then I sincerely hope you achieve your ambition to settle in New Zealand – the land of the long white cloud.

Good luck.

16
Kiwispeak

Every country is blessed with its own slang language and New Zealand is no different. Had we known words that crop up in every day conversation before arriving in the country we may have prevented some short-lived moments of misunderstanding! This list is by no means complete as many words not included here have the same meaning as in the UK and some are simply unprintable! However, it does provide a reasonable insight to the most commonly used terms and may amuse you anyway.

across the ditch
across the other side of the Tasman Sea

ANZAC   Australia and New Zealand Army Corps

arvo   afternoon

awesome   excellent

bach   small holiday home (North Island)

bench   kitchen counter

bludger   sponger

bogan   person from a lower class or background

budgie smugglers
tight, brief swimming trunks

bush   dense area of forest and scrub

carked it   died

chilly bin   insulated picnic box

chippies   crisps

chocka   full up

chocolate fish chocolate covered marshmallow shaped like a fish
(given as a reward)

choice   fantastic

chook   chicken

chunder   vomit

cocky   farmer

college   secondary school

cow spanker   farmer

cracker   very good

crib   small holiday home (South Island)

crook   sick or poorly

cuz   cousin

dag   comedian or joker

dairy   local corner shop

ding   dent on a car

dub-dub-dub Kiwi version of www (as in the internet)

dunny   toilet

eh (pronounced 'ay')
used to emphasise a question, 'That was a great game of
rugby, eh?'

fair go	be reasonable
feed	meal
fizz boat	small powerboat
flat tack	flat out or full speed
flog	steal
footie	rugby (never soccer!)
g'day	hello
give it heaps	try your hardest
gold	brilliant, fantastic
good as gold	no problem or good job
greasies	fish and chips
gumboots	wellington boots
handle	large glass of beer
hard case	strong or wicked personality
hard yakka	hard work
hen fruit	eggs
hongi	Maori greeting by pressing noses together
hoon	boy-racer
hottie	hot water bottle
hui	gathering or conference
ice block	ice lolly
jandals	flip-flops

judder bar	speed bump
jug	kettle
kai	food (Maori)
Kia Ora	hello (Maori)
kina	sea urchin (Maori)
kindy	nursery or pre-school (kindergarten)
lamington	sponge cake covered in coconut
lollies	sweets
long drop	outdoor toilet
lurgy	cold or flu
manus	idiot or fool
mint	excellent or good quality
morning or **afternoon tea**	tea break
mountain oysters	lambs' testicles
munted	broken beyond repair
O.E.	overseas experience
old 'uns	parents
op shop	second-hand shop
pack a sad	upset or broken, 'The car battery has packed a sad'.
pakeha (pak-ee-ha)	non-Maori person

pash	kiss
pattie	beefburger
pav	pavlova - a Kiwi icon!
piss	alcohol
plonked	drunk
plot	grave
pom	British person (derived from Prisoner of Her Majesty)
pottle	punnet
pozzie	position or place
primo	good
rack off	go away
rark up	get angry
rellies	relatives
Rice Bubbles®	Rice Krispies®
root	intercourse
rough as guts	coarse
route	direction (but pronounced 'raute' so not to be confused with root!)
sammies	sandwiches
scab	scrounge
scarfie	university student
schooner	small glass of beer

scungy	run down or worn out
section	land for building on
shickered	drunk
smoko	tea break
snag	sausage
snarlers	sausages
sook	softy or scaredy cat
state house	council house
sticky beak	nosey neighbour
stiff bickies	hard luck
stubbie	bottle of beer
sunnies	sunglasses
sweet as	OK
tiki tour	take the scenic route or long way round
tin arse	lucky
tinny	lucky (also a small aluminum boat)
togs	swimsuit or bathing costume
too right	exactly
tramping	hiking
turps	alcohol (and turpentine!)
ute	pick-up truck

wasted   drunk

whanau (faa-now)
               family (Maori)

wop-wops   very remote location

yeah right!   oh really

17

EVENT PLANNER

The Event Planner has been compiled by recalling the experiences of our family and in no way should be considered as a comprehensive list of every action to be addressed.

The tabulation is not necessarily in order of priority or action, as it is intended for use solely as an *aide-memoir* to assist you with the emigration process.

Subject	Target date	Date complete	Comment
FAMILY ISSUES			
Discuss concept with family			
Determine major issues			
Determine education needs			
Estimate total costs involved			
Decide if emigration is viable			
JOB RESEARCH			
Research Skills Shortage lists			
Investigate job options			
Determine salary level			
In area of possible employment:			
Research schooling facilities			
Research housing market			
Research road/rail links			
Research climate			
Research local amenities			
VISA ACTIONS			
Determine possible visa category			
Check points required			
Complete Points Indicator Form			
Conduct critical assessment of eligibility/feasibility			
Investigate other options (if required)			
NEXT STAGE			
Submit EOI if sufficient points have been scored			
Response from NZIS			YES or NO decision
Determine emigration date			You should have a date to work towards, but make it realistic

Subject	Target date	Date complete	Comment
DOCUMENTATION			
Order visa applications			
Apply for A4 birth certificates			
Apply for police certificates			
Investigate nearest medical examiner			
Arrange medical examination			
Check validity of passports and renew if necessary			
Complete visa applications			
Despatch to NZIS London			Registered post is strongly recommended
HOUSE ISSUES			
Design and construct spidergram			
Investigate house market and determine target sale date			
Select removal company			
Discuss options for potential removal date			
Commence house sort			
Determine items to go and those to stay/donate			
Order skip for rubbish removal			
Investigate unlocking of DVD players/systems			
Investigate network capability of mobile phones			
Include UK 2/4 way adaptors in container inventory			
Deep clean garden tools and furniture			If applicable
Deep clean sports equipment			
Check TV licence expiry and investigate renewal options			

Subject	Target date	Date complete	Comment
INSURANCES			
Investigate validity of endowment policy with mortgage provider			If applicable. Cancellation earlier rather than later may be financially beneficial
Check cover of life insurance and arrange cancellation as necessary			Some cover may be available for journey to NZ
Cancel home contents			When container leaves the house
Cancel car insurance			
Cancel buildings insurance			
Cancel consumer insurance			
CREDIT AND LOYALTY CARDS			
Settle outstanding debt(s) and cancel			
Inform company of emigration and removal from database			
Cancel loyalty cards			
Claim any rewards			Before container leaves for NZ
UTILITY BILLS			
Arrange settlement method			
Final payment dates for:			
Gas			
Water			
Electricity			
Council Tax			
BANK ACCOUNTS			
Determine if UK account is still necessary			
Arrange for six-monthly statements if required			
Open NZ bank account			
Cancel standing orders and direct debits			
Set up transfer arrangements to NZ account			

Subject	Target date	Date complete	Comment
PENSIONS AND BENEFITS			
Suspend pension contributions			Options for transfer to NZ to be investigated after emigration
Inform pension provider with contact details when known			
Inform Benefit Agency(s) of emigration date			
INLAND REVENUE			
Inform Inland Revenue of emigration date			
Outstanding tax liabilities to be completed if applicable			
PETS			
Contact DEFRA for latest regulations			
Arrange testing schedule with vet			Early contact is necessary to ensure testing meets timescale
Contact transit kennel and discuss provisional dates			
Plan flight date to work in with NZ house plan			
TRAVEL			
Investigate potential flight dates			
Research cost-effective travel			Home to airport
Determine clothing needs			Seasonal variation between UK and NZ
Arrange suitable amount of NZ currency			
Collate travel file with all relevant documents			
Investigate and book NZ accommodation			Hotel/motel/home and duration

Index

adaptors 50, 177
All Blacks 7, 138
Antarctic 5, 159

barbecue 4, 6
betting 140
bio-security 51, 81

car culture 128
car insurance 129, 178
Christmas decorations 52
climate 5, 121
conversion rate 5, 135
culture shock 19
customs 81
CV 117

decision making 11, 23, 145
double taxation 16, 60
drink-driving 127
driving licence 125
DVD player 47, 177

earthquakes 136
eating 140, 155
economy 4
electrical appliances 46, 50
emigrate 11
employers 24, 29
employment 23, 109–118
environment 6, 20
exchange rate 14, 118, 163
Expression Of Interest (EOI) 27
extension leads 50

fees 34, 67, 103, 114
fishing 6, 117
flying 2, 13, 73, 78
freezer 50, 95
fridge 50, 95

garden furniture 51
golf 52, 139
gross income 14–16
Gross Sales Tax (GST) 53

heaters 50
hi-fi 48
highways 130
hospital 45, 110, 119

Immediate Skills Shortage List (ISSL)
    111
immigrants 25, 73, 109
immigration 12, 23–36, 75
income 14–18, 60
industry 4, 18, 112
Inland Revenue Department (IRD) 16
insurance 15, 42, 47, 54
interest rates 26, 58
internet 88
inventory 45

job hunting 114
job market 23, 109
job offer 25, 29, 102
job vacancies 112

lifestyle 6, 17, 71, 117
Long Term Skill Shortage List (LTSSL)
    110

markets 8
medical 34–37, 106, 113, 119, 177
medical certificates 34
medical conditions 35
medical waiver 35
Ministry of Agriculture and Forestry
    (MAF) 49–53, 67, 75, 81
mobile phones 51, 177
MOT 53, 129
multi-region codes 48

newspapers 8, 88
New Zealand Immigration Service (NZIS) 24–37, 176
NZ army 115
NZ dollar 14, 62

occupational registration 113
ozone layer 5, 136

parliament 1, 23
passports 35, 75, 177
pensions 62, 164
permanent residency 36
petrol stations 68, 131
points indicator 27, 176
police certificates 33, 177
politics 11, 18
pubs 139

qualifications 25, 106, 110–116
quality of life 12, 24
quarantine 51, 53, 71
Quick Check 27

radiators 50
radio 48, 138
rain 5, 135–136
removal company 43, 177
residency application 30, 34
road code 126, 132

salary 4, 18, 24, 29, 111, 118, 176
schools 102–105, 136
seasons 9, 74, 135
shopping 8
SIM cards 51
Skill Shortage Lists 25, 109–111
Skilled Migrant 26–29
skills 25, 99, 109, 115–116, 176

social 6–7, 108
social sciences 99
speed cameras 130
speed limit 130
sports equipment 52, 177
stereo 48
supermarkets 8, 58, 63, 141

tailgating 131
tax codes 13
taxation 13–17, 60, 164
taxes 13, 106
television 46
temperature 5, 135
trade 4
tumble dryer 49, 164
TV licence 54, 177

used vehicles 52–53
UV 5, 136

vacancies 25, 112
vacuum cleaners 52
VCR 46–47
vineyards 142
Virkon S® 52
visa 23–37
volcanic 2, 142

wages 15–18, 119
Waitangi 1
washing machine 49, 164
watershed 139
weather 5, 135
welcome 6
wines 4, 142
workforce 23–24, 29

zero tolerance 130